OCR Anthology for Latin GCSE 2027–2028

The following titles are available from Bloomsbury for the OCR specifications in Latin and Greek

Cicero *pro Roscio Amerino*: A Selection, with introduction, commentary notes and vocabulary by Neil Treble

OCR Anthology for Latin AS and A Level Shorter Prose Authors, covering the prescribed texts by Nepos, Tacitus and Apuleius, with introduction, commentary notes and vocabulary by Katharine Radice and Stuart R. Thomson

OCR Anthology for Latin AS and A Level Shorter Verse, covering the prescribed texts by Lucretius, Tibullus and Ovid, with introduction, commentary notes and vocabulary by John Godwin

OCR Anthology for Latin GCSE 2027–2028, covering the prescribed texts by Pliny the Younger, Aulus Gellius, Apuleius, Ovid and Virgil, with introduction, commentary notes and vocabulary by Tim Chambers and Declan Lawell

OCR Anthology for Classical Greek GCSE 2027–2028, covering the prescribed texts by Herodotus, Lysias, Homer and Euripides, with introduction, commentary notes and vocabulary by Christopher Burnand and Andy Mylne

OCR Anthology for Classical Greek AS and A Level: 2026–2028, covering the prescribed texts by Aristophanes, Herodotus, Homer, Lucian, Plato and Sophocles, with introduction, commentary notes and vocabulary by Matthew Barr, John Claughton, Benedict Gravell, Rowena Hewes, Ellice Hetherington and Stuart R. Thomson

Virgil *Aeneid* IV: A Selection, with introduction, commentary notes and vocabulary by John Storey

Supplementary resources for these volumes can be found at
www.bloomsbury.com/OCR-editions-2026-2028

Please type the URL into your web browser and follow the instructions to access the Companion Website. If you experience any problems, please contact Bloomsbury at onlineresources@bloomsbury.com

OCR Anthology for Latin GCSE 2027–2028

Edited by
*Tim Chambers and
Declan Lawell*

BLOOMSBURY ACADEMIC
LONDON • NEW YORK • OXFORD • NEW DELHI • SYDNEY

BLOOMSBURY ACADEMIC

Bloomsbury Publishing Plc, 50 Bedford Square, London, WC1B 3DP, UK
Bloomsbury Publishing Inc, 1385 Broadway, New York, NY 10018, USA
Bloomsbury Publishing Ireland, 29 Earlsfort Terrace, Dublin 2, D02 AY28, Ireland

BLOOMSBURY, BLOOMSBURY ACADEMIC and the Diana logo are trademarks of Bloomsbury Publishing Plc

First published in Great Britain 2025

Copyright © Tim Chambers and Declan Lawell, 2025

Tim Chambers and Declan Lawell have expressed their right under the Copyright, Designs and Patents Act, 1988, to be identified as Authors of this work.

Cover design: Terry Woodley
Cover image: Krikkiat/Shutterstock

All rights reserved. No part of this publication may be: i) reproduced or transmitted in any form, electronic or mechanical, including photocopying, recording or by means of any information storage or retrieval system without prior permission in writing from the publishers; or ii) used or reproduced in any way for the training, development or operation of artificial intelligence (AI) technologies, including generative AI technologies. The rights holders expressly reserve this publication from the text and data mining exception as per Article 4(3) of the Digital Single Market Directive (EU) 2019/790.

Bloomsbury Publishing Plc does not have any control over, or responsibility for, any third-party websites referred to or in this book. All internet addresses given in this book were correct at the time of going to press. The author and publisher regret any inconvenience caused if addresses have changed or sites have ceased to exist, but can accept no responsibility for any such changes.

A catalogue record for this book is available from the British Library.

A catalog record for this book is available from the Library of Congress.

ISBN: PB: 978-1-3504-2448-7
       ePDF: 978-1-3504-2449-4
       eBook: 978-1-3504-2450-0

Typeset by RefineCatch Limited, Bungay, Suffolk
Printed and bound in Great Britain by Bell and Bain Ltd, Glasgow

For product safety related questions contact productsafety@bloomsbury.com.

To find out more about our authors and books visit www.bloomsbury.com and sign up for our newsletters.

CONTENTS

Preface vii
How to Use This Book viii
Discussing Literary Style ix
Latin Verse Metre xiv
Technical Terms xvi

Prose Literature A 1
    Pliny the Younger (*Letters* IX.33) 1
    Aulus Gellius (*Attic Nights* V.14) 13

Prose Literature B 26
    Apuleius (*Metamorphoses* Book V, 21–5 and 26–7) 26

Verse Literature A 55
    Ovid (*Metamorphoses* IV.55–166) 55

Verse Literature B 77
    Virgil (*Aeneid* II.1–56 and 195–253) 77

OCR Latin GCSE Defined Vocabulary List 101

Endorsement statement

The teaching content of this resource is endorsed by OCR for use with specification GCSE Latin (9-1) (J282).

All references to assessment, including assessment preparation and practice questions of any format/style, are the publisher's interpretation of the specification and are not endorsed by OCR.

This resource was designed for use with the version of the specification available at the time of publication. However, as specifications are updated over time, there may be contradictions between the resource and the specification, therefore please use the information on the latest specification and Sample Assessment Materials at all times when ensuring students are fully prepared for their assessments.

Endorsement indicates that a resource is suitable to support delivery of an OCR specification, but it does not mean that the endorsed resource is the only suitable resource to support delivery, or that it is required or necessary to achieve the qualification.

OCR recommends that teachers consider using a range of teaching and learning resources based on their own professional judgement for their students' needs. OCR has not paid for the production of this resource, nor does OCR receive any royalties from its sale. For more information about the endorsement process, please visit the OCR website.

PREFACE

This edition is designed to support the teaching of OCR's GCSE Latin Prose and Verse texts for 2027–28. It assumes that students will be familiar with the grammar and syntax items prescribed in the OCR specification and the OCR Defined Vocabulary List (printed at the end of this book for reference).

At the same time, we are very aware that reading unadapted texts after limited experience of Latin is a stiff challenge for the student (and indeed the teacher, if they are not a Latin specialist). Our edition therefore aims primarily to help readers understand what the Latin means. The facing page notes give the meanings of unfamiliar vocabulary and attempt to explain how the Latin fits together grammatically, with translations of the more difficult phrases.

As well as testing a student's understanding of the meaning of the Latin, OCR's GCSE papers also include questions on the literary style of the authors. For reasons of space, our notes make only limited reference to literary effects, but we have included a section on 'Discussing Literary Style' with examples taken from the texts, along with questions on each section of text designed to stimulate thought and classroom discussion. We hope that the edition will enable students not only to enjoy the stories but also to appreciate the quality of the authors' writing.

We would like to record our thanks to Alice Wright and her team at Bloomsbury, and the anonymous reviewers who have made helpful comments along the way.

Declan Lawell
Tim Chambers
July 2024

Bibliography

For further reading, the following more advanced commentaries may be helpful to teachers or students:

Fifty Letters of Pliny, ed. A. N. Sherwin-White, Oxford University Press, 1966.
Pliny the Younger: Complete Letters, trans. P. G. Walsh, Oxford University Press, 2006.
Apuleius: Cupid and Psyche, ed. E. J. Kenney, Cambridge University Press, 2008.
Apuleius, Metamorphoses V: A Selection, ed. S. Thompson, Bloomsbury, 2018.
Aeneidos Liber Secundus, ed. R. G. Austin, Oxford University Press, 1964.
The Aeneid of Virgil, Books 1–6, ed. R. D. Williams, Macmillan, 1972.
Virgil, Aeneid Book II: A Selection, ed. D. Jones, Bloomsbury, 2023.
Ovid: Metamorphoses Books I–IV, ed. D. E. Hill, Aris and Phillips, 1985.
Ovid's Metamorphoses Books 1–5, ed. W. S. Anderson, University of Oklahoma Press, 1997.
Reading Ovid: Stories from the Metamorphoses, ed. P. Jones, Cambridge University Press, 2007.

HOW TO USE THIS BOOK

Starting to read a literary text in the original Latin is always a challenging step. This book tries to help you do this confidently in a number of ways.

1. There are two levels of introduction:
    (i) A specific introduction to your author and the genre of writing.
    (ii) '**The story so far . . .**' or, for the prose authors, an '**Introduction**' to help you set the extract you are reading in context, so that you know what's going on. At the end of your text there may also be a '**What happens next**' section, if the story continues.

    Other reference pages you may find useful include tips on how to discuss literary style, a list of technical terms, a discussion of Latin verse metre and the GCSE word list at the back.

2. **Text pages** (on the left-hand side).
    (i) A heading in *italics* at the top of each page gives an overview.
    (ii) **Names and places:** these explain the names and places mentioned in the text.
    (iii) **Question boxes**: these are designed to help you think more deeply about the content and style of the Latin. Some of the questions may not have a single right or wrong answer; don't worry if you can't answer them all.
    (iv) **Vocabulary boxes**: these contain a list of words from the set GCSE vocabulary relevant to the page of text you are about to read.
        - If you have already learned the GCSE vocabulary list, use this to revise from before you translate.
        - If you are still working on the GCSE vocabulary list, look these words up before you begin.

3. **Notes pages** (on the right-hand side).

    Vocabulary and translation help is arranged line by line. Try not to use this support until you have attempted to work out for yourself what the Latin means.

    (i) Help is given on the meaning of words likely to be unfamiliar to you. Help with words in the GCSE list may also be given, especially if they have a slightly different meaning in this instance from the one you are used to or are in a less familiar form.

(ii) Unfamiliar words that have appeared already may not be translated when they appear subsequently, but you may be directed back by a line reference to an earlier usage.

(iii) Latin words used in the text are in bold.

DISCUSSING LITERARY STYLE

Whenever we read great authors, they impress us not only by *what* they say but *how* they say it. At GCSE, examiners ask questions on the set texts which require answers on the authors' literary style as well as the meaning of the Latin.

This may involve discussing an author's *choice* of words, such as the use of an unusual or particularly powerful word, for example when Aeneas, speaking to Dido about the fall of Troy (*Aeneid* II.3), describes his grief as *infandum* ('unspeakable').

Or it may involve commenting on the *position* of words. Because Latin is an inflected language in which meaning is conveyed not by the order of the words (as in English) but by their grammatical forms, Latin authors regularly placed words in a sentence for particular effect. In the example quoted above, *infandum* is emphasized by its placement at the start of its clause: *infandum, regina, iubes renovare dolorem* ('unspeakable, queen, is the grief you order me to renew').

For reasons of space, the facing page commentary notes make only limited reference to matters of literary style – the notes are designed primarily to help you work out what the Latin means. But it may be helpful for you to have the list of literary techniques which follows below, each with examples from the texts being studied. The list is by no means exhaustive, but these are some of the main ways in which authors add power to their writing.

When discussing a literary effect it is usually not enough merely to identify it (e.g. 'there is alliteration of *m* in line 32') without explaining what the effect is designed to achieve (e.g. 'the alliteration of *m* in <u>m</u>olem <u>m</u>irantur draws our attention to two key words – they suggest the huge size of the wooden horse and the amazement of the Trojans').

Where the literary terms below are used in the commentary notes, they appear with an asterisk (*).

alliteration: the repetition of consonants at the beginning of words – this may be coincidental but writers often used it deliberately to draw attention to particular words or phrases, or to suggest the sound of something:

- *haec tibi identidem semper <u>c</u>avenda <u>c</u>ensebam* (Apuleius 62)
  I was advising you to be always on your guard against these things

- *fit <u>s</u>onitus <u>s</u>pumante <u>s</u>alo* (Virgil 71)
  there was a sound as the salt-sea spumed
- *multum <u>m</u>iseri <u>m</u>eus illiusque parentes* (Ovid 101)
  o most wretched parents, mine and his

anaphora: the repetition of the same word in successive phrases – the effect is to emphasize it:

- *<u>hoc</u> altero die, <u>hoc</u> tertio, <u>hoc</u> pluribus* (Pliny 23)
  this happened on the second day, on the third day, on more days
- *<u>hic</u> Dolopum manus, <u>hic</u> saevus tendebat Achilles* (Virgil 29)
  here was where the band of Dolopians were, here was where wild Achilles pitched his tent
- *vota tamen <u>tetigere</u> deos, <u>tetigere</u> parentes* (Ovid 110)
  her prayers, however, touched the gods, touched the parents

apostrophe: when a speaker turns away to address a character or place not present:

- *o patria, o divum domus Ilium et incluta bello / moenia Dardanidum!* (Virgil, 103–4)
  o homeland, o Troy, home of the gods, and walls of the Trojans famous in war!
- *o quicumque sub hac habitatis rupe leones* (Ovid 60)
  o you lions who live under this rock

assonance: the repetition of vowel sounds, sometimes to reflect the meaning:

- *insonu<u>ere</u> cav<u>ae</u> gemitumque ded<u>ere</u> cav<u>ernae</u>* (Virgil 53)
  the hollow caverns (of the wooden horse) echoed and gave a groan

asyndeton: the omission of connective words such as 'and' or 'but':

- *haec tu qua miseratione, qua copia deflebis ornabis attolles!* (Pliny 44)
  with what compassion [and] with what eloquence will you bewail, embellish, [and] elevate these events

chiasmus: word order in which the second half of a phrase reverses the word-order of the first (ABBA):

- *vesanae libidinis et invidiae noxiae* (Apuleius 96)
  mad lust and destructive jealousy

- *fracti bello fatisque repulsi* (Virgil 13)
  broken by war and driven back by fate
- *hinc Thisbe, Pyramus illinc* (Ovid 17)
  Thisbe on this side, Pyramus on that

consonance: the repetition of consonant sounds:

- *videt o<u>m</u>niu<u>m</u> feraru<u>m</u> <u>m</u>itissi<u>m</u>am dulcissi<u>m</u>amque bestia<u>m</u>* (Apuleius 13)
  she saw the beast, the gentlest and sweetest of all wild beasts
- *pe<u>ct</u>ora quorum inter flu<u>ct</u>us arre<u>ct</u>a* (Virgil 68)
  their breasts, raised among the waves

ellipsis: the omission of a word which is easily understood from the context, sometimes to create an especially short, pithy sentence:

- *delphinus rursus ad tempus* (Pliny 20)
  the dolphin [appeared] on time again
- *audacem faciebat amor* (Ovid 42)
  love made [her] bold

enclosing word order: the placement of a word/words inside other words, sometimes to mirror the meaning:

- *<u>purpureo</u> tingit pendentia mora <u>colore</u>* (Ovid 73)
  it tinged the hanging fruits with purple colour

enjambment: running the final word of a phrase over a line-end in verse to give it added emphasis at the start of the following line:

- *post ipsum auxilio subeuntem ac tela ferentem
  corripiunt* (Virgil 78–9)
  after, as he came to help and bore arms, they seized him
- *non aliter quam cum vitiato fistula plumbo
  scinditur* (Ovid 68–9)
  just as when a pipe with damaged lead is split

historic present: the use of a present tense to describe past events – the effect is to make the narrative more vivid and dramatic as if it is happening in the present (sometimes also called the 'vivid present'):

- *nec mora; ferventi moriens e vulnere traxit.
  ut iacuit resupinus humo, cruor <u>emicat</u> alte* (Ovid 66–7)
  there was no delay; dying he drew (the sword) from the boiling wound. When he lay on his back on the ground, blood <u>spurts out</u> high

hyperbaton: where a word is placed at a distance from another word with which it is to be taken (e.g. an adjective-noun combination) – the effect is often to emphasize both words

- *visaque detectae fidei colluvie* (Apuleius 48)
  with the filth of his betrayed trust having been seen
- *infandum, regina, iubes renovare dolorem* (Virgil 3)
  unspeakable, queen, is the grief you order me to renew

juxtaposition: putting words next to each other (e.g. to balance or contrast them):

- *adnatat nanti* (Pliny 26)
  (the boy) swims towards the swimming (dolphin)
- *'una duos' inquit 'nox perdet amantes'* (Ovid 54)
  'one night' he said 'will destroy two lovers'

metaphor: when a person/thing is described with imagery relating to something else (as distinct from simile):

- *uterumque armato milite complent* (Virgil 20)
  they filled the womb with armed soldiers (the wooden horse is described as a womb pregnant with men)

personification: the description of an inanimate object as if it were a person:

- *'invide' dicebant 'paries, quid amantibus obstas?'* (Ovid 19)
  'hateful wall', they said, 'why do you obstruct lovers?'

polyptoton: the repetition of a word in different forms or cases for emphasis:

- *ego et leo in eadem specu eodemque et victu viximus* (Gellius 48–9)
  the lion and I lived in the same cave and on the same food
- *quoque magis tegitur, tectus magis aestuat ignis* (Ovid 10)
  and the more it was hidden, the more the hidden fire blazed
  (*magis tegitur tectus magis* is also a good example of chiasmus)

polysyndeton: the repeated use of connective words such as 'and' or 'or':

- *unus leo corporis impetu et vastitudine terrificoque fremitu et sonoro* (Gellius 12–13)
  one lion, because of its power and vast size, and its terrifying and loud roar
- *involvens umbra magna terramque polumque / Myrmidonumque dolos* (Virgil 113–14)
  covering with its great darkness both the earth and the sky and the treachery of the Greeks

rhetorical question: asking a question without expecting a reply:

- *tametsi quid poetae cum fide?* (Pliny 4)
  although what concern does a poet have with reliability?
- *'miseri, quae tanta insania, cives?'* (Virgil 42)
  'wretched citizens, what great madness is this?'
- *'invide' dicebant 'paries, quid amantibus obstas?'* (Ovid 19)
  'jealous wall,' they said, 'why do you obstruct lovers?'

simile: when a person/thing is described as if it is like (Latin *similis*) something else (as opposed to metaphor):

- *aestu pelagi simile maerendo fluctuat* (Apuleius 2)
  in her grieving she is tossed to and fro as if on the tide of the sea
- *qualis mugitus, fugit cum saucius aram / taurus* (Virgil 85–6)
  (his shouts were) like the bellowing when a wounded bull has fled from an altar
- *exhorruit aequoris instar / quod tremit, exigua cum summum stringitur aura* (Ovid 135–6)
  she shuddered like the sea which trembles when its surface is ruffled by a small breeze

tricolon: the grouping of three words or phrases (if each word/phrase increases in length it is sometimes known as an 'ascending' tricolon):

- *ante lectuli pedes iacebat <u>arcus</u> et <u>pharetra</u> et <u>sagittae</u>* (Apuleius 30–1)
  before the feet of the bed lay his bow, quiver and arrows
- *<u>o patria</u>, <u>o divum domus Ilium</u> et <u>incluta bello / moenia Dardanidum</u>!* (Virgil 103–4)
  o fatherland, o Troy, home of the gods and the walls of the Trojans famous in war!

LATIN VERSE METRE

The principles of Latin verse are very different from English verse, which is largely based on stressed and unstressed syllables. Instead, Latin used combinations of long/heavy and short/light syllables. Epic poetry like Homer's *Iliad* and *Odyssey* and Virgil's *Aeneid* was traditionally composed in lines consisting of six metrical units (or 'feet'). Ovid also used this metre for his *Metamorphoses*. It is called the 'hexameter' from the Greek words for six (ἕξ – hex) and measure (μέτρον – metron).

Knowledge of metre is not required for GCSE, but you cannot really gain a full appreciation of the poetry of Virgil and Ovid without it. Latin poetry was often written to be recited and heard rather than read, and the music of the hexameter sometimes conveys meaning all by itself. A brief guide is therefore included here for those who would like to know more.

The two basic units of the hexameter are the 'dactyl' (a long/heavy syllable followed by two short/light syllables) and the 'spondee' (two long/heavy syllables). When a line of verse is 'scanned' (i.e. annotated) with the syllable lengths/weights, a dactyl is marked – ∪∪ (dum-di-di) and a spondee – – (dum-dum).

Each hexameter line has six metrical units (or 'feet'). The fifth foot is almost always a dactyl, which creates the impression that one line is accelerating towards the next. The last foot can be a spondee or a trochee (– ∪).

The full scheme is therefore:

```
   1      2      3      4      5      6
 – ∪∪ | – ∪∪ | – ∪∪ | – ∪∪ | – ∪∪ | – ∪
  – –  |  – –  |  – –  |  – –  |       |  – –
```

There is not space here for a full explanation of what constitutes a long/heavy or a short/light syllable, or how poets used a word-break in the middle of a line to create a slight pause (the 'caesura'), but in general:

- diphthongs (combinations of vowels like *ae*) are long;
- final *-a* and final *-e* are usually short (the ablative singular of a first declension noun is a significant exception);
- final *-i* and final *-o* are usually long;
- final *-os*, *-as*, and *-es* are usually long;
- a short syllable before two consonants is counted as long, even if they are split across two words;
- a final vowel or *-um/-am/-em* may be cut ('elided') if followed by a word beginning with a vowel or *h* (as in the first example below).

LATIN VERSE METRE

A-level candidates learn how to mark the syllables of a line as short (∪) or long (–) and show how they combine to create a line of six feet (in the case of the hexameter). At GCSE it will be enough for you to be aware of two particular metrical effects:

- a high proportion of dactyls (– ∪∪) gives a line a fast-moving feel and may suggest rapid action or a tone of lightness/happiness;
- a line with a lot of spondees (– –) has a slow, heavy feel and may suggest a sense of doom or ill omen.

Compare and contrast the following examples from our selection:

Virgil
Mostly spondees:

– –/ – –/– –/   – –/ – ∪∪/– –
aut hoc inclusi lign(o) occultantur Achivi
or enclosed in this piece of wood Greeks are hiding (line 45)

The reference is to the ominous possibility that the Trojan horse is a trap.

Mostly dactyls:

– ∪∪/ – ∪ ∪/– ∪∪/– ∪ ∪/ – ∪ ∪/– –
sub pedibusque deae clipeique sub orbe teguntur
they hide under the feet of the goddess and the circle of her shield (line 9)

The rapid movement created by the five dactyls may suggest the speed with which the snakes slither away into Minerva's temple.

Ovid
Mostly spondees:

– –/ – – /––/ – – / – ∪∪/– –
ex aequo captis ardebant mentibus ambo
their minds were captured and they were both burning equally (line 8)

The heavy spondees may suggest the seriousness of the love between Pyramus and Thisbe.

Mostly dactyls:

– ∪ ∪/– ∪∪/ – ∪∪/– ∪∪/ – ∪ ∪/– ∪
vidit ebur vacuum, 'tua te manus' inquit 'amorque
– ∪∪
perdidit'
(after) she saw the ivory without its sword, she said 'your hand and love have destroyed you' (lines 94–5)

The sequence of five dactyls speeds up the action as Thisbe suddenly realizes what has happened to Pyramus.

TECHNICAL TERMS

ablative absolute: a combination of a noun or pronoun with a participle, when they are not the subject or object of the main verb in the sentence.

causal ablative: the use of noun in the ablative case to show the cause of something (e.g. *vastitudine* = 'because of its huge size').

conditional: a sentence describing a possibility – it usually begins with *si* = 'if' or *nisi* = 'if . . . not', 'unless'.

contraction: the shortening of a word (e.g. *Danaum* = *Danaorum*, *audisse* = *audivisse*).

dactyl: in verse, a combination of a heavy/long syllable with two short/light syllables.

elision: in verse, when a final vowel or *-m* is cut off ('elided') if it is followed by a word beginning with a vowel or *h*.

gerund: a noun formed from a verb (e.g. *navigandi* studium = enthusiasm for sailing).

hexameter: the standard metre of epic poetry (e.g. Homer, Virgil, Ovid in his *Metamorphoses*).

historic infinitive: the use of an infinitive instead of a perfect tense to describe a past event (e.g. *narrare* = 'they told') – Pliny is fond of this device.

instrumental ablative: the use of a noun in the ablative case to show by what something is done (e.g. *urere flammis* = 'to burn with flames').

partitive genitive: the use of the genitive case to describe a part of the whole (e.g. *multum viae* = much of the way).

possessive dative: the use of the verb 'to be' with a noun or pronoun in the dative case as a way of saying that someone has something (e.g. *est mihi* = 'there is to me', i.e. 'I have').

spondee: in verse, two heavy/long syllables together.

Prose Literature A

2027–28 Prescription

Pliny, *Letters* IX.33, omitting *quamquam non est opus . . . sunt vera minuantur*.
Aulus Gellius, *Attic Nights* V.14, omitting *sed in his . . . sui venditator*.

Pliny the Younger

Gaius Plinius Caecilius Secundus, better known as Pliny the Younger, was born in 61 CE in modern Como in Italy. After his father died, he was raised and educated by his uncle, Pliny the Elder. When his uncle died rescuing the victims of the eruption of Mount Vesuvius (79 CE), Pliny inherited his uncle's estate. Pliny was also a trained public speaker who prepared for a career in law. He became very successful indeed and embarked on a political career, going through all the political ranks up to holding the consulship in 100 CE. He later served as the governor of Bithynia (in modern Turkey) until his death in around 113 CE.

His career was a remarkable achievement given that he gained promotion under a range of different emperors, including the maligned autocrat, Domitian. He is mostly known for his *Letters*, which give a fascinating insight into the daily and political life of Rome and Italy at the time. He also composed a grand speech (the *Panegyricus*) in honour of the emperor Trajan.

Introduction

Pliny's *Letters* (*Epistulae*) are a collection of letters written in ten books. Although many of the letters are private on the surface, and addressed to personal friends, Pliny nevertheless did intend the letters to be published for a wide readership. Pliny deals with a vast range of themes in Books I–IX: everything from how he spent time on holiday, the difficulties of hiring a schoolteacher, the eruption of Mount Vesuvius, the gardens in his villas, and ghost stories. The story in this anthology involves a dolphin which appeared on the coast of Africa and proceeded to interact with the human population.

Book X of the *Letters* deals with his administration of the province of Bithynia and his interactions with the emperor Trajan, including his deliberations on how to deal with Christians. Numerous other famous Roman personalities appear in his letters, including the historians Tacitus and Suetonius, the poet Martial, and of course his uncle, Pliny the Elder, a noted natural historian and admiral in the Roman navy. Despite the fact that Pliny intended to publish his letters, they are nonetheless a fascinating insight into the more everyday and commonplace aspects of Roman life in contrast to other more historical writings.

Pliny tells his friend, the poet Caninius, that he has a marvellous story to relate to him which could be a suitable topic for his poetry.

C. PLINIVS CANINIO SVO S.

incidi in materiam veram sed simillimam fictae, dignamque isto laetissimo altissimo planeque poetico ingenio; incidi autem, dum super cenam varia miracula hinc inde referuntur. magna auctori fides: tametsi quid poetae cum fide? is tamen auctor, cui bene vel historiam scripturus credidisses. est in Africa Hipponensis colonia   5
mari proxima. adiacet navigabile stagnum; ex hoc in modum fluminis aestuarium emergit, quod vice alterna, prout aestus aut repressit aut impulit, nunc infertur mari, nunc redditur stagno.

(Pliny *Letters* IX.33.1–2)

Names and places
Caninius, -i (m): Caninius (a poet and friend of Pliny).

Africa, -ae (f): Africa (Roman province of North Africa).

Hipponensis, -e: of Hippo, the ancient name of the modern city of Bizerte in Tunisia.

Dolphins
Pliny's uncle, Pliny the Elder, also wrote a similar story about dolphins. See *Natural History*, IX.26–7 for a shorter version of this same story.

Q. Why do you think Pliny begins this letter by discussing questions of truth and reliability, and the relationship between history and poetry?

Q. Pliny asks *quid poetae cum fide* ('what concern do poets have with reliability?'). What do you think he means by this?

GCSE vocabulary: *altus, bene, cena, credo, cum, dum, ex, flumen, hic, iaceo, in, is, laetus, magnus, mare, modus, nunc, proximus, qui, quid, refero, scribo, tamen.*

C. PLINIVS CANINIO SVO S. – A capital letter U was often written as V in Roman script, while S. is an abbreviation for *salutem*; Gaius Plinius Caninio suo salutem [dicit]: a standard form of address in Roman letters; **salutem [dicit]** – 'sends greetings'; **suo** – a short version of *suo amico* (the poet Caninius Rufus was a friend of Pliny).

1. **incido, -ere, incidi** – I come across; **materia, -ae (f)** – a subject; **verus, -a, -um** – true; **similis, -is, -e** – similar; **fictus, -a, -um** – made up, fiction; **dignus, -a, -um** + the ablative *ingenio* – worthy of; **iste, ista, istud** – that: *isto* agrees with *ingenio*.

2. **laetissimo** – *laetus* here is best translated as 'rich' or 'luxuriant'; **plane** – clearly, evidently; **poeticus, -a, -um** – poetic; **ingenium, -i (n)** – talent; **autem** – however.

3. **super cenam** – 'over dinner'; **varius, -a, -um** – different; **miraculum, -i (n)** – marvel; **hinc inde** – to and fro; **auctor, -oris (m)** – author, source: *auctori* is a possessive dative: 'the author/source has . . .'; the source here could possibly be Pliny's uncle, Pliny the Elder, or else someone speaking at the dinner.

4. **fides, fidei (f)** – reliability (agreeing with *magna*); **tametsi** – although; **poeta, -ae (m)** – poet; **quid poetae cum fide?** – 'what concern does a poet have with reliability?'; **cui** – dative of *qui* going with *credidisses*; **vel** – even.

5. **historia, -ae (f)** – history; **cui . . . credidisses** – 'whom you would have trusted'; **scripturus** – 'if you were about to write'; **est** – 'there is'; **colonia, -ae (f)** – colony or Roman settlement (Hippo was originally settled in by Roman veteran soldiers).

6. **adiaceo, -ere** – I lie next to (*adiacet*: 'lies next to the colony'); **navigabilis, -e** – navigable, translate as 'on which boats can sail'; **stagnum, -i (n)** – lake, lagoon; **in modum** – 'like'.

7. **aestuarium, -i (n)** – estuary, channel; **emergo, -ere** – I flow out; **quod** – which (it refers back to *aestuarium*); **vice alterna** – 'alternately'; **prout** – as; **aestus, -us (m)** – tide; **aut . . . aut** – either . . . or; **reprimo, -ere, repressi** – I force back.

8. **impello, -ere, impuli** – I drive forward; **infertur** – 'flows into'; **redditur** – 'returns': both verbs are to be taken with *quod*. The verbs are literally passive but best translated actively.

While boys were swimming in the lake, a dolphin appeared.

omnis hic aetas piscandi navigandi atque etiam natandi studio tenetur, maxime pueri, quos otium lususque sollicitat. his gloria et virtus altissime provehi: victor ille, qui longissime ut litus ita simul natantes reliquit. hoc certamine puer quidam audentior ceteris in ulteriora tendebat. delphinus occurrit, et nunc praecedere puerum nunc sequi nunc circumire, postremo subire deponere iterum subire, trepidantemque perferre primum in altum, mox flectit ad litus, redditque terrae et aequalibus. serpit per coloniam fama; concurrere omnes, ipsum puerum tamquam miraculum adspicere, interrogare audire narrare.

10

15

(Pliny *Letters* IX.33.3–5)

> Q.   What impression do you have of the boys in this passage?
> Q.   Pliny uses the historic infinitive on many occasions here – what effect does this have?
> Q.   How does Pliny express the excitement of what is happening?

> **GCSE vocabulary:** *ad, altus, atque, audio, ceteri, eo, etiam, fero, hic, ille, ipse, ita, iterum, longus, maxime, mox, narro, navigo, nunc, omnis, pono, primus, puer, -que, qui, quidam, reddo, relinquo, sequor, simul, teneo, terra, ut, virtus.*

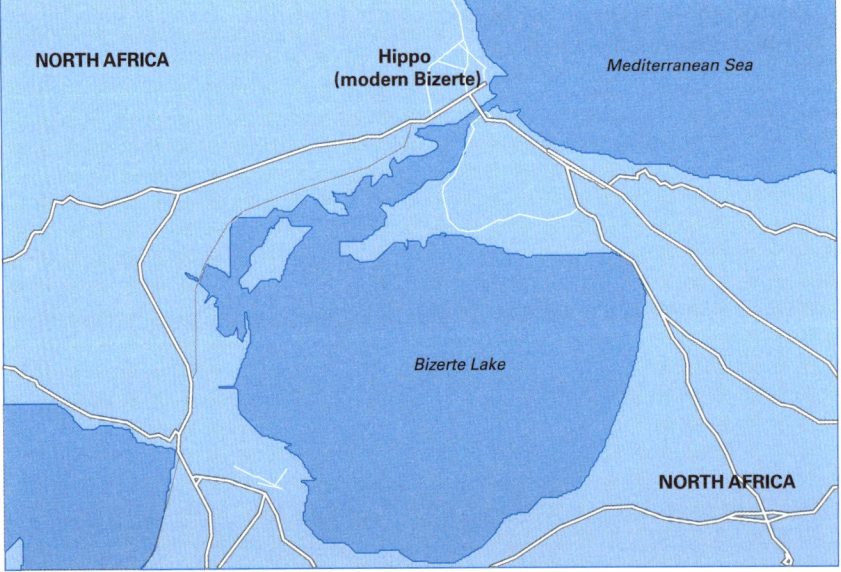

Figure 1 *Map of Hippo.*

9   hic – here (i.e. in the estuary); **aetas, -atis (f)** – age; **omnis aetas** – 'people of all ages'; **piscor, -ari** – I fish; **navigo, -are** – I sail; **nato, -are** – I swim; **studium, -i (n)** – enthusiasm, eagerness; **piscandi, navigandi, natandi** – these are gerunds in the genitive after the ablative *studio*: literally 'in eagerness of fishing, sailing, swimming', but best translated as 'eagerness for fishing etc.'

10 **otium, -i (n)** – leisure; **lusus, -us (m)** – sport; **sollicito, -are** – I attract, I entice: the subjects of *sollicitat* are *otium* and *lusus*; **his** – 'their' (possessive dative plural of *hic, haec, hoc*); **gloria, -ae (f)** – boast.

11 **his gloria et virtus** – understand a verb such as *est*: literally, 'it is their boast and heroism/courage', but best taken as 'it is their heroic boast to swim far out'; **provehor, -vehi** – I swim far out; **altissime** – 'into the deepest water'; **victor, -oris (m)** – winner; **ille** – understand *est ille*; **ut . . . ita** – both . . . and; **litus, -oris (n)** – shore.

12 **natantes** – the swimmers; **certamen, -inis (n)** – contest, competition; **audentior** – more daring; **in ulteriora** – 'further out'.

13 **tendo, -ere** – I head out; **delphinus, -i (m)** – dolphin; **occurro, -ere, occurri** – I meet; **praecedo, -ere** – I go before; *praecedere* and *sequi* are historic infinitives to be translated as perfect tense verbs, with *delphinus* as the subject.

14 **circumeo, -ire** – I go round; **postremo** – at last; **subeo, -ire** – I go under: translate *subire* here as 'takes on its back'; **depono, -ere** – I put down; the verbs are all historic infinitives.

15 **trepido, -are** – I am afraid; **trepidantem** – understand *puerum* here; **perfero, perferre** – I carry; **primum** – firstly; **in altum** – 'into deep water'; **mox** – then (here); **flecto, -ere** – I turn back; **litus, -oris (n)** – shore.

16 **reddo, reddere** – I restore, I return to; **aequalis, -is (m)** – companion, friend; **serpo, -ere** – I spread; **colonia, -ae (f)** – colony; **fama, ae (f)** – rumour, story; **concurro, -ere** – I hurry together, I flock together: *concurrere* and the rest of the verbs in this passage are historic infinitives.

17 **tamquam** – as if; **miraculum, -i (n)** – marvel, prodigy; **adspicio, -ere** – I look at; **interrogo, -are** – I ask questions.

18 **narrare** – 'they spread the story'.

The dolphin continues to come back.

postero die obsident litus, prospectant mare et si quid est mari simile. natant pueri, inter hos ille, sed cautius. delphinus rursus ad tempus, rursus ad puerum. fugit ille cum ceteris. delphinus, quasi invitet et revocet, exsilit mergitur, variosque orbes implicat expeditque. hoc altero die, hoc tertio, hoc pluribus, donec homines innutritos mari subiret timendi pudor. accedunt et adludunt et adpellant, tangunt etiam pertrectantque praebentem. crescit audacia experimento. maxime puer, qui primus expertus est, adnatat nanti, insilit tergo, fertur referturque, agnosci se amari putat, amat ipse; neuter timet, neuter timetur; huius fiducia, mansuetudo illius augetur. nec non alii pueri dextra laevaque simul eunt hortantes monentesque. 20

25

(Pliny *Letters* IX.33.5–7)

> Q. *timendi pudor*: why did the local community feel shame over their fear in this passage?
> Q. *crescit audacia experimento*: 'boldness grew with experience' – what does Pliny mean by this?

GCSE vocabulary: *ad, alius, alter, amo, cum, dies, eo, et, etiam, fero, fugio, hic, homo, hortor, ille, inter, invito, ipse, mare, maxime, moneo, puer, primus, puto, -que, qui, re-, se, sed, si, simul, sub, timeo, voco.*

19 **posterus, -a, -um** – the following; **obsideo, -ere** – I besiege, I take over, I occupy; **litus, -oris (n)** – shore; **prospecto, -are** – I look out over; **quid** = *aliquid* – anything; **similis, -e** – similar; **si quid est mari** – literally, 'if there is anything similar to the sea', translate as 'any waters resembling the sea' (Pliny is referring to the lake).

20 **nato, -are** – I swim; **ille** – he (i.e. the boy to whom the dolphin first appeared); **cautus, -a, -um** – cautious (*cautius* is the comparative adverb); **delphinus, -i (m)** – dolphin; **rursus** – again (supply a verb, e.g. 'appeared'); **ad tempus** – on time.

21 **rursus** – supply a verb, e.g. 'went towards'; **quasi** (+ subjunctive) – as if; **invitet et revocet** – understand 'the boy' as the object of these verbs.

22 **exsilio, -ire** – I leap up; **mergo, -ere** – I dive; **mergitur** – the passive is used in a reflexive sense: 'it dived'; **varius, -a, -um** – different; **orbis, -is (m)** – circle; **implico, -are** – I weave, I coil; **expedio, -ire** – I uncoil, I unfold; **variosque orbes implicat expeditque** – literally 'it wove and unwove different circles', translate as 'it curled and uncurled itself into different shapes'; **hoc** – supply a verb: 'this happened'.

23 **pluribus** (i.e. *diebus*) – 'on several other days'; **donec** – until; **innutritus, -a, -um** – nourished, brought up on; **mari** – by the sea (instrumental ablative).

24 **subeo, -ire** – I come over, I enter: the subject of *subit* is *timor* and the object is *homines innutritos*; **timendi pudor** – 'shame at being afraid'; **accedo, -ere** – I approach; **adludo, -ludere** – I play with; **adpello, -are** – I speak to; **tango, -ere** – I touch.

25 **pertrecto, -are** – I stroke: the object of these verbs is the dolphin; **praebeo, -ere** – I offer; understand *delphinum* with the participle *praebentem* and a verb such as *se tangi*: 'the dolphin offering itself to be touched'; **cresco, -ere** – I increase; **audacia, -ae (f)** – boldness; **experimentum, -i (n)** – experience.

26 **maxime** – especially; **experior, -iri, expertus sum** – I experience; **adnato, -are** – I swim to; **nanti** – 'to the dolphin swimming'; **insilio, -ire** – I leap onto; **tergum, -i (n)** – back.

27 **fertur referturque** – 'he was carried out to sea and brought back again'; **agnosco, -ere** – I recognize; **putat** – the word order is: (the boy) *putat se agnosci [et] amari*; **neuter, neutra, neutrum** – neither.

28 **huius** – his (the boy's); **fiducia, -ae (f)** – trust; **mansuetudo, -inis (f)** – tameness; **illius** – its (the dolphin's); **augeo, -ere** – I increase; **nec non** – and also;

29 **dextra laevaque** – on the right and on the left; **eunt** – 3rd person plural of *eo, ire*; **monentes** – advising (i.e. the other boys were advising the boy).

A second dolphin appears.

ibat una (id quoque mirum) delphinus alius, tantum spectator et   30
comes. nihil enim simile aut faciebat aut patiebatur, sed alterum illum
ducebat reducebat, ut puerum ceteri pueri. incredibile, tam verum
tamen quam priora, delphinum gestatorem collusoremque puerorum
in terram quoque extrahi solitum, harenisque siccatum, ubi
incaluisset in mare revolvi.   35

(Pliny *Letters* IX.33.7–8)

> Q. In his version of the story, Pliny the Elder says that the dolphin in question came to land out of love for humans, and then died as its skin dried. How is this different from Pliny the Younger's version here? Which version do you think is more likely?

GCSE vocabulary: *alius, ceteri, comes, duco, enim, eo, ex, facio, ille, in, is, mare, nihil, patior, puer, quoque, re-, sed, terra, traho, ubi, ut.*

Figure 2 *An engraving depicting a young boy riding on a friendly dolphin.*
Photo: Universal History Archive/Contributor/Getty Images.

30 **una** (adverb) – alongside, together with; **mirus, -a, -um** – wonderful (understand a verb such as *erat* with *id*); **tantum** (adverb) – only; **spectator, -oris (m)** – spectator, observer.
31 **aut . . . aut** – either . . . or.
32 **incredibilis, -e** – unbelievable (understand *est*) followed by an indirect statement (see next line); **verus, -a, -um** – true.
33 **tam verum tamen quam** – add in a word such as 'but' before this phrase; **tam . . . quam** – as . . . as; **priora** – previous events; in the following lines, Pliny uses the accusative and infinitive construction: *incredibile [est] delphinum solitum [esse] trahi . . . revolvi*: 'it is unbelievable . . . that the dolphin . . .'; **gestator, -oris (m)** – carrier; **collusor, -oris (m)** – companion, playmate; **puerorum** – Pliny is perhaps exaggerating here as the dolphin seems only to have let one boy onto its back.
34 **solitum** = *solitum esse* ('was accustomed') followed by *trahi*; **harena, -ae (f)** – sand; **harenis** – on the sand; **sicco, -are** – I dry; **ubi** – when.
35 **incalesco, -ere, incalui** – I get hot; **revolvo, -ere** – I roll back (the passive infinitive *revolvi* is used in a reflexive sense: 'to roll itself back'. The same applies to *extrahi*).

The dolphin is put to death.

constat Octavium Avitum, legatum proconsulis, in litus educto religione prava superfudisse unguentum, cuius illum novitatem odoremque in altum refugisse, nec nisi post multos dies visum languidum et maestum, mox redditis viribus priorem lasciviam et solita ministeria repetisse. confluebant omnes ad spectaculum magistratus, quorum adventu et mora modica res publica novis sumptibus atterebatur. postremo locus ipse quietem suam secretumque perdebat: placuit occulte interfici, ad quod coibatur. haec tu qua miseratione, qua copia deflebis ornabis attolles! vale.

40

(Pliny *Letters* IX.33.9–11)

Names and places
Octavius Avitus, -i (m): Octavius Avitus (deputy governor of North Africa).

> Q. What is your opinion regarding the actions of Octavius Avitus and of the local townspeople in this passage? Are their actions justifiable?
>
> Q. 'It was decided that the object of these crowds be killed' – why does Pliny speak about the dolphin and the people in this way? Is it significant that Pliny uses the neuter *quod* for the dolphin and the impersonal passive *coibatur* for the crowds of people?

GCSE vocabulary: *ad, altus, dies, duco, et, fugio, hic, ille, interficio, ipse, locus, mox, multus, nisi, novus, omnis, post, qui, -que, -re, res, reddo, suus, tollo, tu, video.*

36 **constat** – it is known: this verb governs the following four infinitives (*superfudisse, refugisse, visum [esse], repetisse*) in the accusative and infinitive construction; **legatus, -i (m)** – legate (a deputy of the governor); **proconsul, -is (m)** – proconsul (governor of a Roman province); **litus, -oris (n)** – shore; **educto** – referring to the dolphin, from **educo, -ere, eduxi, eductus** – I lead out: here translate *educto* as 'as it lay'.

37 **religio, -onis (f)** – superstition; **pravus, -a, -um** – depraved, abnormal; **religione prava** – causal ablative: 'because of . . .'; **superfundo, -ere, -fudi** – I pour over; **unguentum, -i (n)** – ointment; **cuius** – of which (i.e. the ointment); **illum** – it (i.e. the dolphin): it is helpful to supply *et* before *illum* since this is the second indirect statement; **novitas, -atis (f)** – newness, here = 'unusual treatment'.

38 **odor, -oris (m)** – odour, fragrance; **in altum** – to the deep sea; **refugio, -ere, -fugi** – I flee from; **refugisse** – the object is *odorem* (the subject being the dolphin); **nec** – and not; **nisi post multos dies** – 'until many days later'; **visum** = *visum esse*.

39 **languidus, -a, -um** – lacking energy, listless; **maestus, -a, -um** – unhappy, sad; **vires, virium (f pl)** – strength; **redditis viribus** – ablative absolute; **prior, prioris** – previous; **lascivia, -ae (f)** – playfulness.

40 **solitus, -a, -um** – usual; **ministerium, -i (n)** – service; **repeto, -ere, repetii** – I resume; **repetisse** = perfect active infinitive (the subject is again the dolphin); **confluo, -ere** – I flock to; **omnes** – agrees with *magistratus*; **spectaculum, -i (n)** – sight.

41 **magistratus, -us (m)** – magistrate (i.e. political and civil officer); **quorum** – referring to the magistrates; **adventus, -us (m)** – arrival; **mora, -ae (f)** – lodging, staying: magistrates visiting a town in a province would expect to be housed and entertained by the local community; **modicus, -a, -um** – small (agreeing with *res publica*); **res publica** – community, colony.

42 **sumptus, -us (m)** – expense; **attero, -ere** – I wear down, I weaken; **postremo** – finally; **quies, -etis (f)** – tranquillity, peace.

43 **secretum, -i (n)** – seclusion, privacy; **perdo, -ere** – I lose; **placuit** – it was decided; **occultus, -a, -um** – secret; **coeo, coire** – I come together, I gather: **placuit occulte interfici, ad quod coibatur** – literally 'it was decided that the thing (supply *id*) to which (*ad quod*) there was a gathering (*coibatur*) should be killed secretly', this can be translated as 'it was decided that the object of these crowds should be killed secretly'.

44 **haec** – these events; **qua** – 'with what . . .!'; **miseratio, -onis (f)** – compassion; **copia, -ae (f)** – eloquence; **defleo, -ere** – I bewail, I lament; **orno, -are** – I embellish; **attollo, -ere** – I elevate; **vale** – goodbye.

Aulus Gellius

Aulus Gellius was, like Pliny, a Roman lawyer who lived from around 125 CE until some time after 180 CE. Most of the information we know about him is derived from his own writings. He seems to have been brought up in Rome, but also received an education in Athens. It was during his time there in Athens, in Attica, that he collected the materials for his essay collection, the *Attic Nights*.

Returning to Rome, Gellius was promoted to the office of praetor which led him to be involved in many court cases. Gellius had an important influence on several later writers including Augustine and one of the other authors in this anthology, Apuleius.

Introduction

The *Attic Nights* (*Noctes Atticae*) is a collection of essays which Gellius arranged in order to entertain his readers. They were based on Gellius' own notes in a kind of sketchbook he kept in which he recorded interesting facts and stories he came across. A broad range of topics is covered, spanning the areas of philosophy, history, language and literature, and they have helped to preserved numerous stories from the ancient world which might otherwise have been lost, including the story of Androcles and the lion in this anthology. The collection is called *Attic Nights* since they were composed during the long winter nights Gellius spent in Attica, Greece.

Figure 3 *The Circus Maximus in Rome.*
Photo: Getty Images.

Gellius introduces the reader to Apion who is his source for this story about Androcles and the lion and, quoting Arion, describes the scene in the Circus Maximus.

Apion, qui 'Plistonices' appellatus est, litteris homo multis praeditus rerumque Graecarum plurima atque varia scientia fuit. eius libri non incelebres feruntur, quibusomnium ferme, quae mirifica in Aegypto visuntur audiunturque, historia comprehenditur. hoc autem, quod in libro Aegyptiacorum quinto scripsit, neque audisse neque legisse, sed ipsum sese in urbe Roma vidisse oculis suis confirmat. 5

'in Circo Maximo,' inquit, 'venationis amplissimae pugna populo dabatur. eius rei, Romae cum forte essem, spectator,' inquit, 'fui. multae ibi saevientes ferae, magnitudines bestiarum excellentes, omniumque invisitata aut forma erat aut ferocia. sed praeter alia omnia leonum,' 10 inquit, 'immanitas admirationi fuit praeterque omnes ceteros unus. is unus leo corporis impetu et vastitudine terrificoque fremitu et sonoro, toris comisque cervicum fluctuantibus animos oculosque omnium in sese converterat.'

(*Attic Nights* V.14, 1–2, 4, 5–9)

Names and places

Apion Plistonices (m): Apion (his surname is Plistonices) was a Hellenized Egyptian (i.e. an Egyptian influenced by the spread of Greek culture) who worked in the first half of the first century CE; he wrote books on grammar as well as commentaries on Homer.

Aegyptus, -i (f): Egypt.

Aegyptiaca, -orum (n pl): The Wonders of Egypt (the title of Apion's work).

Circus Maximus, -i (m): the Circus Maximus, a stadium in Rome used for chariot racing, wild beast hunts, and other games.

Q. How does Gellius present Apion as a reliable source?
Q. What does Gellius say to convey the sense of excitement and anticipation at being at the games in the Circus Maximus?

GCSE vocabulary: alius, animus, atque, audio, ceteri, corpus, do, fero, forte, hic, homo, ibi, ipse, is, liber, multus, omnis, -que, qui, res, Roma, scribo, se, sed, sum, unus, urbs, video.

1   appello, -are – I call; litterae, -arum (f pl) – letters, learning, scholarship; *litteris* agrees with *multis*; praeditus, -a, -um – versed in, endowed with.

2   plurima atque varia scientia fuit – *scientia* is ablative of description, literally 'he was with very great and varied knowledge': translate as 'he had …'.

3   inceleber, -bris, -bre – without fame; non incelebres – a double negative and understatement from Gellius: Apion's books are said to be 'not without fame', i.e. 'famous'; feruntur – *fero* here means 'I say' or 'I acknowledge'; quibus – 'in which'; omnium – the subject is historia, ae (f) – an account, a history; ferme – almost; mirificus, -a, -um – wonderful; the word order is *historia fere omnium mirifica quae …*: best translated as 'an account of almost all the wonders which …'.

4   viso, -ere – I see; comprehendo, -ere – I contain; hoc – supply a noun, e.g. 'this story, this event'; autem – however.

5   *Aegyptiaca, -orum* (n pl) – *The Wonders of Egypt* (the name of Apion's book); quintus, -a, -um – fifth; neque … neque – neither … nor; the infinitives *audisse* (= a contraction of *audivisse*), *legisse*, and *vidisse*, all come after *confirmat*.

6   sese – an emphatic form of the reflexive pronoun *se*; oculus, -i (m) – eye; confirmo, -are – I make clear, I affirm.

7   inquit – 'he (Arion) says'; venatio, -onis (f) – wild beast hunt; amplus, -a, -um – lavish, splendid; pugna, -ae (f) – fight; venationis amplissimae pugna – literally 'a fight of a very lavish wild beast hunt', best translated as 'a very lavish fight with wild beasts'; populus, -i (m) – the people.

8   spectator, -oris (m) – eyewitness (+ *eius rei*).

9   saevio, -ire – I am savage; fera, -ae (f) – wild beast; magnitudo, -inis (f) – size; bestia, -ae (f) – beast; excellens, -entis – exceptional; understand the verb *erant* with *ferae* and *magnitudines*; magnitudines bestiarum excellentes – literally, 'exceptional sizes of beasts', translate as 'beasts of exceptional size'; omnium – 'of all' (i.e. the wild beasts).

10 invisitatus, -a, -um – uncommon, unseen before; aut … aut – either … or; forma, -ae (f) – appearance; ferocia, -ae (f) – ferocity; praeter – above, more than; leo, leonis (m) – lion.

11 immanitas, -atis (f) – vast size; admirationi fuit – was amazing (the subject is *immanitas*, and *admirationi* is dative: literally 'was for amazement'); praeter – above, more than.

12 impetus, -us (m) – power, force; vastitudo, -inis (f) – huge size: *impetu* and *vastitudine* are causal ablatives ('because of …') which explain why the lion attracted so much attention; terrificus, -a, -um – terrifying; fremitus, -us (m) – roar; sonorus, -a, -um – loud.

13 torus, -i (m) – muscle; comae, -arum (f pl) – mane; cervices, cervicum (f pl) – neck; fluctuo, -are – I ripple (regarding the lion's muscles), I stream, I flow (regarding the mane); animos – (here) attention; *fremitu, toris*, and *comis* are causal ablatives: 'because of …'; oculus, -i (m) – eye; omnium – of everyone.

14 sese – emphatic form of *se*; converto, -ere, converti – I turn, I draw.

Androcles and the lion recognize each other.

'introductus erat inter complures ceteros ad pugnam bestiarum datus   15
servus viri consularis; ei servo Androclus nomen fuit. hunc ille leo
ubi vidit procul, repente,' inquit, 'quasi admirans stetit ac deinde
sensim atque placide tamquam noscitabundus ad hominem accedit.
tum caudam more atque ritu adulantium canum clementer et blande
movet hominisque se corpori adiungit cruraque eius et manus prope   20
iam exanimati metu lingua leniter demulcet. homo Androclus inter
illa tam atrocis ferae blandimenta amissum animum recuperat,
paulatim oculos ad contuendum leonem refert. tum quasi mutua
recognitione facta laetos,' inquit, 'et gratulabundos videres hominem
et leonem.'   25

(*Attic Nights* V.14.10–14)

Names and places
Androclus, -i (m): Androcles (this is the Greek form of his name which is more commonly used in English).

> Q. What range of emotions do you think Androcles experienced in this scene?

> **GCSE vocabulary:** *ac, animus, atque, ad, corpus, deinde, do, duco, ceteri, et, facio, hic, homo, iam, ille, inter, is, laetus, manus, moveo, nomen, prope, -que, refero, se, servus, sto, sum, tam, tum, ubi, video, vir.*

15 **introduco, -ere** – I bring in; **complures, -es, -a** – several; **pugna, -ae (f)** – fight; **bestia, -ae (f)** – beast; **datus** – provided, given.

16 **vir consularis** – a man of consular rank (i.e. a man who had completed a term in office as consul).

17 **procul** – from a distance; **repente** – suddenly; **quasi** – as if; **admiror, -ari** – I am amazed.

18 **sensim** – gradually; **placidus, -a, -um** – quiet; **tamquam** – as if; **noscitabundus, -a, -um** – recognizing; **accedo, -ere** – I approach (*accedit* is historic present).

19 **cauda, -ae (f)** – tail; **mos, moris (m)** – manner; **ritus, -us (m)** – fashion, way; **more atque ritu** – 'in the manner and way of . . .'; **adulo, -are** – I show affection; **canis, -is (m/f)** – dog: *canum* is genitive plural with *adulantium*; **clementer** – gently; **blande** – caressingly.

20 **adiungo, -ere** – I bring myself close to; **crus, cruris (n)** – leg; **eius** – his (Androcles'); **prope** – nearly (+ *exanimati*).

21 **exanimatus, -a, -um** – half-dead (*exanimati* is genitive: understand 'of him/ Androcles'); **metus, -us (m)** – fear (*metu* is causal ablative, 'because of his fear'); **lingua, -ae (f)** – tongue (in the ablative here); **leniter** – gently; **demulceo, -ere** – I lick.

22 **atrox, atrocis** – fierce; **fera, -ae (f)** – wild beast; **blandimentum, -i (n)** – a caress; **amitto, -ere, amisi, amissus** – I lose; **animum** – 'his senses'; **recupero, -are** – I recover, I regain.

23 **paulatim** – gradually; **oculus, -i (m)** – eye; **contueor, -eri** – I look at (*ad contuendum* is a gerundive purpose clause); **refero, referre** – I bring, I turn; **quasi** – as if; **mutuus, -a, -um** – mutual, of each other; **recognitio, -onis (f)** – recognition; **mutua recognitione facta** is ablative absolute.

24 **gratulabundus, -a, -um** – 'sharing joyful exchanges'; **videres** – 'you might have seen' (this is a potential subjunctive: the idea is that if you were present, you might have seen this).

Androcles explains to the emperor how he met the lion.

ea re prorsus tam admirabili maximos populi clamores excitatos dicit accersitumque a Caesare Androclum quaesitamque causam, cur illi atrocissimus leo uni parsisset. ibi Androclus rem mirificam narrat atque admirandam. 'cum provinciam,' inquit, 'Africam proconsulari imperio meus dominus obtineret, ego ibi iniquis eius et cotidianis   30
verberibus ad fugam sum coactus et, ut mihi a domino, terrae illius praeside, tutiores latebrae forent, in camporum et arenarum solitudines concessi ac, si defuisset cibus, consilium fuit mortem aliquo pacto quaerere. tum sole medio,' inquit, 'rabido et flagranti specum quandam nanctus remotam latebrosamque in eam me   35
penetro et recondo. neque multo post ad eandem specum venit hic leo debili uno et cruento pede gemitus edens et murmura dolorem cruciatumque vulneris commiserantia.'

(*Attic Nights* V.14.15–19)

Names and places
Caesar, -aris (m): the emperor (this is Gaius Caesar, better known as Caligula): emperors were often known simply as Caesar.

Africa, -ae (f): Africa (North Africa was a Roman province).

> Q.   How do you think Gellius wants the reader to feel about Androcles here?

GCSE vocabulary: *ac, ad, advenio, animus, atque, cibus, clamor, cogo, consilium, cum, cur, dico, dominus, ego, et, hic, ibi, ille, imperium, is, medius, meus, mors, multo, narro, pes, primo, quaero, quidam, res, sum, tam, terra, terreo, tum, unus, ut, venio, vulnus.*

26 **prorsus** – utterly, completely; **admirabilis, -e** – astonishing (*admirabili* agrees with *ea re*); **populus, -i (m)** – the people; **excito, -are** – I raise: *excitatos* = perfect passive infinitive *excitatos esse*; **dicit** – 'he (Apion) says'.

27 **accersitum** (another form of *arcessitum*) = *accersitum esse*, from **arcesso, -ere, -ivi, -itus** – I summon; **quaesitam** = *quaesitam esse* (from **quaero, -ere, quaesivi, quaesitus** – I ask); **causa, -ae (f)** – the reason.

28 **atrox, atrocis** – fierce; **parco, -ere, parsi** (+ dative) – I spare: **(illi) uni** (him alone) is dative after *parsisset*; **ibi** – here translate as 'then'; **mirificus, -a, -um** – wonderful.

29 **admirandus, -a, -um** – amazing; **cum** ('when') goes with *obtineret*; **provincia, -ae (f)** – province; **inquit** – 'he (Androcles) said'; **proconsularis, -e** – proconsular (a proconsul was a magistrate/politician/civil servant who governed a province after having completed a term as a consul).

30 **imperium, -i (n)** – authority, power; **obtineo, -ere** – I hold, I am in charge of; **iniquus, -a, -um** – unjust, undeserved; **eius** – his (i.e. the master's); **cotidianus, -a, -um** – daily.

31 **verber, -eris (n)** – beating, flogging; **fuga, -ae (f)** – flight, fleeing; **sum coactus** = *coactus sum*; **a domino** – take with (*latebrae*) *tutiores* ('safer from my master'); **ut** introduces a purpose clause to explain why Androcles fled to desert locations; the word order is *ut latebrae forent tutiores mihi a domino*.

32 **praeses, praesidis (m)** – ruler; **tutus, -a, -um** – safe; **latebrae, -arum (f pl)** – hiding-place; **forent** is equivalent to *essent* (imperfect subjunctive); **campus, -i (m)** – a plain; **arena, -ae (f)** – desert, sand.

33 **solitudo, -inis (f)** – lonely place; **concedo, -ere, concessi** – I withdraw to; **camporum et arenarum solitudines** – literally, 'the lonely places of the plains and deserts', translate as 'the lonely plains and deserts'; **desum, deesse, defui** – I run out, I am lacking; **consilium fuit** – literally 'the plan was', translate as 'I intended'.

34 **aliquo pacto** – 'in some way or other'; **sol, solis (m)** – the sun; **medius, -a, -um** – at midday; **rabidus, -a, -um** – raging; **flagrans, -antis** – scorching; **sole medio rabido et flagranti** – these are all in the ablative case, translate as 'when the midday sun was . . .'.

35 **specus, -us (f)** – cave; **quandam** – accusative feminine singular of *quidam*; **nanctus** – perfect participle from deponent verb **nanciscor, nancisci, nanctus sum** – I find; **remotus, -a, -um** – remote; **latebrosus, -a, -um** – secluded, full of hiding-places; **eam** – it (the cave); **me penetro, -are** – I make my way into.

36 **recondo, -ere** – I hide; **neque multo post** – not long afterwards; **eandem** (+ *specum*) is feminine accusative singular from *idem* (the same).

37 **debilis; -e** – weak; **cruentus, -a, -um** – bloodstained; **leo debili uno et cruento pede** = *leo uno pede debili et cruento*; **gemitus, -us (m)** – groan; **edo, -ere** – I give out, I make; **murmur, -uris (n)** – moan; **dolor, -oris (m)** – pain.

38 **cruciatus, -us (m)** – suffering; **commiseror, -ari** – I seek pity for (*commiserantia* agrees with *murmura*, and its objects are *dolorem* and *cruciatum*).

Androcles helps the lion and afterwards they live in the same cave.

atque illic primo quidem conspectu advenientis leonis territum sibi et
pavefactum animum dixit. 'sed postquam introgressus,' inquit, 'leo, 40
uti re ipsa apparuit, in habitaculum illud suum, videt me procul
delitescentem, mitis et mansues accessit et sublatum pedem
ostendere mihi et porrigere quasi opis petendae gratia visus est. ibi,'
inquit, 'ego stirpem ingentem vestigio pedis eius haerentem revelli
conceptamque saniem volnere intimo expressi accuratiusque sine 45
magna iam formidine siccavi penitus atque detersi cruorem. illa tunc
mea opera et medella levatus pede in manibus meis posito recubuit et
quievit, atque ex eo die triennium totum ego et leo in eadem specu
eodemque et victu viximus.'

(*Attic Nights* V.14.20–4)

> Q. Do you think this is a credible series of events, or just a made-up story?

GCSE vocabulary: *atque, advenio, animus, atque, dico, dies, ego, et, ex, iam, ibi, idem, ille, ingens, is, magnus, manus, meus, ostendo, pes, peto, postquam, primo, se, sed, sine, suus, terreo, tollo, totus, video, videor, vivo, vulnus.*

39 illic – there; **quidem** – indeed; **conspectus, -us (m)** – sight; **leo, leonis (m)** – lion; **territum** = *territum esse*; **sibi** – his (Androcles').

40 **pavefacio, -ere, -feci, -factus** – I frighten; **pavefactum** = *pavefactum esse*; **introgredior, -gredi, -gressus sum** – I enter; **introgressus** = *introgressus est*.

41 **uti** = *ut* (+ indicative); **uti re ipsa apparuit** – literally, 'as appeared from the thing itself', translate as 'as became clear from what in fact happened'; **habitaculum, -i (n)** – dwelling-place, lair; **procul** – at a distance.

42 **delitesco, -ere** – I hide; **mitis, -e** – gentle; **mansues, -is** – tame; **accedo, -ere, accessi** – I approach.

43 **ostendere** – both this infinitive and *porrigere* follow after *visus est* ('seemed'); **porrigo, -ere** – I stretch out; **quasi** – as if; **ops, opis (f)** – help; **gratia** + genitive of a gerundive (here *petendae*) = purpose clause: 'to, in order to'; **ibi** – then.

44 **stirps, stirpis (f)** – splinter, thorn; **vestigium, -i (n)** – sole (of the lion's paw); **vestigio** = *in vestigio*; **haereo, -ere** – I stick; **revello, -ere, revelli** – I pull out.

45 **concipio, -ere, concepi, conceptus** – (in the passive) I gather, I am collected; **conceptam** – take with *saniem*; **sanies (f)** (accusative *saniem*) – pus; **volnere** = *vulnere*; **intimus, -a, -um** – inside; **volnere intimo** – 'from deep inside the wound'; **exprimo, -ere, expressi** – I squeeze out; **accuratius** – rather carefully.

46 **magna** – agrees with *formidine*; **formido, -inis (f)** – fear; **sicco, -are** – I dry; **penitus** – thoroughly; **detergo, -ere, detersi** – I wipe away; **cruor, -oris (m)** – blood; **tunc** – then.

47 **opera, -ae (f)** – attention, effort; **medella, -ae (f)** – treatment; **illa mea opera et medella** – 'by that effort and treatment of mine' (following after *levatus*); **levo, -are, -avi, -atus** – I relieve; **pede posito** = ablative absolute phrase; **recumbo, -ere, recubui** – I lie down.

48 **quiesco, -ere, quievi** – I go to sleep; **triennium, -i (n)** – three years; **eadem** (agreeing with *specu*) – feminine ablative singular of *idem*; **specus, -us (f)** – cave.

49 **eodem** (agreeing with *victu*) – masculine ablative singular of *idem*; **et** – also; **victus, -us (m)** – food.

Androcles leaves the cave, but is captured and brought to Rome.

'nam, quas venabatur feras, membra opimiora ad specum mihi   50
subgerebat, quae ego ignis copiam non habens meridiano sole torrens
edebam. sed ubi me,' inquit, 'vitae illius ferinae iam pertaesum est,
leone in venatum profecto reliqui specum et viam ferme tridui
permensus a militibus visus adprehensusque sum et ad dominum ex
Africa Romam deductus. is me statim rei capitalis damnandum   55
dandumque ad bestias curavit. intellego autem,' inquit, 'hunc quoque
leonem me tunc separato captum gratiam mihi nunc beneficii et
medicinae referre.'

(*Attic Nights* V.14.25–8)

Names and places
Africa, -ae (f): Africa (a Roman province).

> Q.   What experience do you think Androcles had living with a lion?
> Q.   Why do you think he grew tired of living with the lion?

GCSE vocabulary: *ad, capio, dominus, de, do, duco, ego, ex, habeo, hic, iam, ille, intellego, miles, nam, nunc, proficiscor, qui, quoque, refero, relinquo, Roma, res, sed, statim, tunc, ubi, via, video, vita.*

50 **venor, -ari** – I hunt; **fera, -ae (f)** – beast; **membrum, -i (n)** – part, joint; **opimus, -a, -um** – fat, choice, best; **quas venabatur feras opimiora membra** – although *feras* has taken the accusative case in the relative clause, it is better to translate it as a genitive in English: 'the choicest joints of the beasts which it (the lion) brought'; **membra** is the object of *subgerebat*; **specus, -us (f)** – cave.

51 **subgero, -ere** – I bring; **copia, -ae (f)** – source, supply; **meridianus, -a, -um** – midday; **sol, solis (m)** – sun; **torreo, -ere** – I roast.

52 **edo, -ere** – I eat; **illius** – feminine genitive singular of *ille* (that) agreeing with *vitae*; **ferinus, -a, -um** – wild; **me pertaesum est** – I tired of, I grew weary of (this verb takes the genitive which here is *vitae illius ferinae*).

53 **venatus, -us (m)** – hunting; **leone profecto** = ablative absolute; **ferme** – almost; **triduum, -i (n)** – three days.

54 **permensus** = perfect participle from deponent verb *permetior, -iri* with **viam** = 'having travelled' (literally 'having measured out the way'); **adprehendo, -ere, -prehendi, -prehensus** – I capture; **dominum** – this is the cruel master from whom Androcles had previously escaped.

55 **deduco, -ere, deduxi, deductus** – I take, I lead; **deductus** = *deductus sum*; **rei capitalis damnare** = to condemn to death.

56 **bestia, -ae (f)** – wild beast; **curo, -are, -avi** + gerundive = I have something done: hence, **me rei capitalis damnandum dandumque ad bestias curavit** = 'he had me condemned to death and thrown (literally 'given') to the wild beasts'; **autem** – however.

57 **separo, -are, -avi, -atus** – I separate; **me tunc separato** = ablative absolute: 'after I was separated from it at that time'; **leonem** agrees with **captum** and is accusative in indirect statement after *intellego*; **gratiam refero, referre** = I give thanks: the things one gives thanks for are in the genitive case (here: *beneficii* and *medicinae*); **beneficium, -i (n)** – kindness.

58 **medicinae, -ae (f)** – treatment.

Androcles is given freedom and is gifted with the lion.

haec Apion dixisse Androclum tradit eaque omnia scripta circumlataque tabula populo declarata atque ideo cunctis petentibus dimissum Androclum et poena solutum leonemque ei suffragiis populi donatum. 'postea,' inquit, 'videbamus Androclum et leonem loro tenui revinctum urbe tota circum tabernas ire, donari aere Androclum, floribus spargi leonem, omnes ubique obvios dicere: "hic est leo hospes hominis, hic est homo medicus leonis".' 65

(*Attic Nights* V.14.29–30)

Names and places
Apion, -onis (m): Apion (Gellius' source).

Androclus, -i (m): Androcles.

> Q. Does the ending of this story surprise you in any way?

GCSE vocabulary: *atque, circum, dico, eo, et, hic, homo, is, omnis, peto, poena, postea, scribo, sum, taberna, totus, trado, urbs, video.*

59 **haec** – literally, 'these things', perhaps translate as 'this story'; **trado, -ere** – record, hand down; *tradit* is followed by five infinitives in indirect statement: *dixisse, declarata, dimissum, solutum, donatum* (*esse* should be understood with the last four).

60 **circumfero, -ferre, -tuli, -latus** – I circulate, I carry around; **scripta circumlataque** – understand *haec* ('these things' or 'this story having been. . .'); **tabula, -ae (f)** – tablet; **tabula** = *in tabula*; **declaro, -are** – I make known; **ideo cunctis petentibus** – 'and because everyone was demanding it'.

61 **dimitto, -ere, -misi, -missus** – I free; **poena solvo, -ere, solvi, solutus** – I acquit, I let off from punishment; **ei** – 'to him'; **suffragium, -i (n)** – vote.

62 **populus, -i (m)** – the people; **dono, -are** – I give as a gift: take *leonem* with *donatum (esse)*; **videbamus** is followed by four infinitives (*ire, donari, spargi, dicere*): the 'we' refers to the people.

63 **lorum, -i (n)** – leash, lead; **tenuis, -e** – thin; **revinctum** (agreeing with *leonem*) from **revincio, -ire, revinxi, revinctus** – I tie up; **urbe tota** = *in tota urbe*; **aes, aeris (n)** – money; **donari aere Androclum** – 'Androcles was presented with money'.

64 **flos, floris (m)** – flower; **spargo, -ere** – I shower, I sprinkle; **ubique** – everywhere, anywhere; **obvius, -a, -um** – in the way, presenting oneself; **obvios** (agreeing with *omnes*) – 'everyone who met them'.

65 **leo, leonis (m)** – lion; **hospes, -itis (m)** – friend, host; **medicus, -i (m)** – doctor.

Final questions

- What do the stories of the dolphin, and of Androcles and the lion, tell us about the treatment of animals in ancient Rome?
- Did Androcles deserve to be freed? What is your overall judgement on his character?
- In what ways do both Pliny and Gellius make their stories fascinating to read?
- Do you think there are any differences between the two authors?

Prose Literature B

2027–28 Prescription

Apuleius, *Metamorphoses* Book V, 21 (*at Psyche relicta sola* ...) –25 (... *herbis exposuit*) and 26–7.

Apuleius

All our knowledge about Apuleius comes from what he tells us in his own writings. He was born in Madaura in North Africa around the year 125 CE. His family was considerably wealthy which meant he could gain a good education, including time spent in Athens. Interestingly, Apuleius was a contemporary of one of the other authors in this anthology, Aulus Gellius, who also studied in Athens. He travelled widely and even to Rome where he worked as a public speaker. Returning from Rome, he married a wealthy widow named Pudentilla in Tripoli. This caused some annoyance to her relatives, who prosecuted Apuleius, alleging that he had won over Pudentilla by magic. Apuleius was able to acquit himself in a brilliant defence speech called the *Apology*. It seems Apuleius went on to be a public figure in Carthage into the 160s, but the date of his death is not known.

As well as the *Apology*, a selection of parts of his public speeches has survived in a work called the *Florida*. His main work, however, was a novel which is the only complete Roman narrative to survive to this day. The novel is called the *Metamorphoses* ('the Transformations'), or sometimes *The Golden Ass*. It tells the story of a man named Lucius who, after having an accident while dabbling in magic, gets turned into an ass. Golden in this context means something such as 'splendid' or 'amazing'. The novel contains eleven books (or chapters), and the selection you will read (the story of Cupid and Psyche) comes from Book V.

Apuleius' writings need to be situated in the larger Graeco-Roman world he wrote in. At this time, there was a major revival of the style of writing and speech-making that was at its peak in Greece in the fifth century BCE. Although Apuleius was writing in Latin, his style was greatly influenced by this revival. This genre is notable for its flowery style of language, for making references to literary traditions, and for using vocabulary and grammar that show off as if in a public performance. For example, when Cupid has flown away from Psyche, Apuleius will talk about him making himself distant on the oars of his wings – his language is rich, metaphorical and exuberant.

His writing is also fun – and that is what he wrote in the preface of his book: 'Reader, pay attention – you will enjoy yourself!' The novel is full of strange and fantastic stories which make for a gripping read. There are, however, other more important themes which run throughout the book. These include the theme of curiosity: Lucius, and indeed Psyche, constantly get in trouble because they cannot control their curiosity. There are also religious and philosophical themes – at the end of the novel, Lucius is transformed back from an ass to a human, and is initiated into the rites of the goddess Isis. We shall also see references to Platonic philosophy in the language used to describe Psyche in our selection.

The story so far

The story of Cupid and Psyche is a story within a story. In *The Golden Ass*, the young traveller, Lucius, has become intrigued by magic. When he tries to practise some sorcery himself, it all goes wrong and he ends up being transformed into an ass. As an ass, he has many strange and wonderful adventures, until finally he is transformed back into human form by eating rose petals sacred to the goddess Isis. He is then initiated into the mysteries of Isis' religion.

Our GCSE text begins at the point when Lucius (in the form of an ass) has been stolen by a band of robbers and is being held in a cave. There is also a girl present named Charite. She has been kidnapped by the robbers on the day of her wedding and is being held captive in the cave. When the robbers go out one day, Charite and Lucius are left with an old woman. Seeing that Charite is upset about what may happen to her, the old woman decides to tell her a story: the story of Cupid and Psyche.

Once upon a time, there was a beautiful girl named Psyche. She was the child of a king and queen in an unnamed city, and had two other sisters. Psyche was so beautiful that people thought she was as beautiful as Venus, perhaps even her daughter. Venus was enraged that people even stopped worshipping in her temples. Venus then sent her son, Cupid, to get revenge by making Psyche fall in love with someone ugly and lowly. Cupid accidentally pricked himself with one of his own arrows and therefore, when he saw Psyche, he immediately fell in love with her. Disobeying his mother, he took her to his enchanted palace where they lived together. Eventually, she became pregnant. The only condition imposed on Psyche by Cupid was that she could never look upon his face or know his true identity, since he remained hidden from her sight.

When Psyche's two sisters visited, they were filled with envy at the lifestyle Psyche was leading in the palace filled with splendour and riches. They asked questions about her husband, and Psyche (who had never seen him) ended up giving contradictory reports to the sisters. The sisters then, out of their wicked jealousy, made up a story that in fact she had married a horrible monster who was waiting to devour Psyche and her child who was soon to be born. Shocked by and believing this news, Psyche listened to a plan the sisters had devised for Psyche to light a lamp and to cut the throat of the monster with a blade. The sisters departed, assuring Psyche that they were waiting to help her. Psyche now prepared to slay her husband, Cupid, whom she believed was a deadly beast.

Psyche has been persuaded by her two wicked sisters to murder her husband, Cupid. Psyche experiences a range of emotions as she prepares.

at Psyche relicta sola, nisi quod infestis Furiis agitata sola non est, aestu pelagi simile maerendo fluctuat, et, quamvis statuto consilio et obstinato animo, iam tamen facinori suas manus admovens, adhuc incerta consilii titubat multisque calamitatis suae distrahitur affectibus. festinat differt, audet trepidat, diffidit irascitur; et, quod   5
est ultimum, in eodem corpore odit bestiam, diligit maritum. vespera tamen iam noctem trahente, praecipiti festinatione nefarii sceleris instruit apparatum. nox aderat et maritus advenerat primusque Veneris proeliis velitatus altum in soporem descenderat.

(*Metamorphoses* V.21.3–5)

Names and places
Psyche, Psyches (f): Psyche, the young girl at the centre of the story. Her name in Greek means 'soul'.

Furiae, -arum (f pl): the Furies, goddesses of vengeance. They are usually named as three, Tisiphone, Megaera and Alecto, and were responsible for punishing sinners or evildoers. They were usually depicted with snakes for their hair.

Venus, Veneris (f): Venus, the Roman goddess of love (here = the act of making love).

Q.   Why do you think Apuleius mentions the Furies here? (line 1)
Q.   Do you think Apuleius wants the reader to feel sympathy for Psyche?
Q.   How does Apuleius show the confusion and turmoil Psyche experiences in this passage?
Q.   *odit bestiam, diligit maritum* (line 6): explain the paradox in this phrase.

GCSE vocabulary: *adsum, audeo, altus, animus, consilium, corpus, descendo, festino, iam, idem, manus, maritus, moveo, multus, nisi, nox, proelium, relinquo, scelus, solus, suus, tamen, traho.*

1   **at** – but; **sola** – Psyche is alone now as her sisters have left her; **nisi quod** – 'except that'; **infestus, -a, -um:** hostile; **agito, -are** – I drive.

2   **aestus, -us (m)** – tide; **pelagus, -i (n)** – sea; **simile** – like, as if; **aestu pelagi simile** – 'as if on the tide of the sea'; **maereo, -ere** – I grieve; **maerendo** – 'in her grieving'; **fluctuo, -are** – I am tossed to and fro; **quamvis** – although; **statuo, -ere, statui, statutus** – I decide, I make (a decision or plan).

3   **obstino, -are** – I am determined; **statuto consilio et obstinato animo** – take these as ablative absolute phrases with *quamvis*; **facinus, facinoris (n)** – deed, crime; **admovens** ('applying') is a compound verb (*ad* + *moveo*): its object is *suas manus*.

4   **adhuc** – still; **incertus, -a, -um** – unsure (followed here by the genitive word *consilii*); **titubo, -are** – I waver, I am unsteady; **calamitas, -atis (f)** – disaster; **distraho, distrahere** – literally 'I drag apart': here in the passive = 'I am torn'.

5   **affectus, -us (m)** – emotion: *multis* agrees with *affectibus*; **differo, differre** – I delay; **trepido, -are** – I fear; **diffido, diffidere** – I despair; **irascor, irasci, iratus sum** – I get angry.

6   **ultimus, -a, -um** – last, furthest, worst; **quod est ultimum** – 'what is worst': the idea seems to be that this is the hardest or worst thing Psyche experiences, namely hating the beast that she thinks is the (unseen) husband she loves; **eodem** – ablative of *idem* (because of *in* + the ablative) and agreeing with *corpore*; **odi, odisse** – I hate; **bestia, -ae (f)** – beast; **diligo, -ere** – I love.

7   **vespera, -ae (f)** – evening; **vespera** agrees with *trahente*, an ablative absolute phrase with *noctem* as object; **praeceps, praecipitis** – headlong, rash; **festinatio, -onis (f)** – haste, speed; **nefarius, -a, -um** – wicked.

8   **instruo, -ere** – I prepare; **apparatus, -us (m)** – equipment; **advenerat** – a compound verb (*ad* + *venio*).

9   **velitor, -ari, velitatus sum** – I skirmish, I fight; **primusque Veneris proeliis velitatus** – 'having first skirmished in the battles of love': Venus' name is used here to represent lovemaking. The idea of love as warfare was a common theme in Latin literature; **sopor, -oris** (m) – sleep.

Psyche gains strength, but is shocked to find out the true identity of her husband.

tunc Psyche, et corporis et animi alioquin infirma, fati tamen saevitia   10
subministrante viribus roboratur, et prolata lucerna et adrepta
novacula sexum audacia mutavit. sed cum primum luminis oblatione
tori secreta claruerunt, videt omnium ferarum mitissimam
dulcissimamque bestiam, ipsum illum Cupidinem formonsum deum
formonse cubantem. cuius aspectu lucernae quoque lumen hilaratum   15
increbruit et acuminis sacrilegi novaculam paenitebat. at vero Psyche
tanto aspectu deterrita et impos animi, marcido pallore defecta
tremensque desedit in imos poplites et ferrum quaerit abscondere,
sed in suo pectore. quod profecto fecisset, nisi ferrum timore tanti
flagitii manibus temerariis delapsum evolasset. iamque lassa, salute   20
defecta, dum saepius divini vultus intuetur pulchritudinem, recreatur
animi.

(*Metamorphoses* V.22.1–5)

Names and places
Cupido, Cupidinis (m): Cupid.

> Q. How does Apuleius emphasize the range of emotions Psyche experiences?
> Q. How many references to vision and light can you find?
> Q. In what ways does Apuleius personify objects in the passage?

GCSE vocabulary: *animus, corpus, deus, dum, facio, iam, ille, ipse, manus, nisi, omnis, quaero, quoque, -que, saepe, sed, suus, tamen, tantus, video.*

10 alioquin – in general; **infirmus, -a, -um** + genitive – weak; **et corporis et animi infirma** – 'weak in both body and soul'; **fatum, -i (n)** – fate; **saevitia, -ae (f)** – cruelty.

11 **subministro, -are** – I supply strength; **saevitia subministrante** – ablative absolute; **vires, virium (f pl)** – strength; **roboro, -are** – I strengthen; **viribus roboratur** – literally 'she is strengthened in strength': translate as 'she increases in strength'; **profero, -ferre, -tuli, -latus** – I bring forth; **lucerna, -ae (f)** – lamp; **adripio, -ere, adripui, adreptus** – I seize.

12 **novacula, -ae (f)** – razor; **prolata lucerna et adrepta novacula** – both are ablative absolute; **sexus, -us (m)** – sex; **audacia, -ae (f)** – boldness, daring; **muto, -are** – I change; **sexum audacia mutavit** – *audacia* is ablative: 'she changes sex in her boldness'; **cum primum** – 'as soon as'; **lumen, -inis (n)** – light; **oblatio, -ionis (f)** – offering.

13 **torus, -i (m)** – bed; **secreta, -orum (n pl)** – secrets; **claresco, -ere, clarui** – I become illuminated (the subject of this verb is *secreta*); **fera, -ae (f)** – wild animal; **mitis, -e** – gentle.

14 **dulcis, -e** – sweet; **bestia, -ae (f)** – beast; **formonsus, -a, -um** – beautiful, handsome; **illum ipsum Cupidinem** – 'Cupid, his very self': this is the first time Cupid is named in the story.

15 **cubo, -are, cubui, cubitus** – I rest, sleep; **aspectus, -us (m)** – sight; **cuius aspectu** – *aspectu* is ablative; *cuius* is genitive singular of the relative pronoun and refers back to Cupid: 'at whose (his) sight'; **hilaro, -are** – I cheer, I gladden.

16 **increbresco, -ere, increbrui** – I increase (the subject of the verb is *lumen*); **acumen, -inis (n)** – sharpness; **sacrilegus, -a, -um** – sacrilegious; **paenitet, paenituit** (+ accusative) – it is a source of regret to: the things regretted go into the genitive case; **at vero** – but indeed; both the lamp and the razor are personified by Apuleius.

17 **deterritus, -a, -um** – terrified; **impos, impotis** (+ *genitive*) – not in control of; **marcidus, -a, -um** – weak; **pallor, -oris (m)** – paleness; **defectus, -a, -um** – overcome; **marcido pallore defecta** – literally 'overcome by weak paleness', translate as: 'overcome with the paleness of weakness'.

18 **tremo, -ere, tremui** – I tremble, I shake; **desido, desidere, desedi, desessus** – I sink down; **imus, -a, -um** – the bottom of; **poples, poplitis (m)** – knee; **ferrum, -i (n)** – iron, weapon, blade; **abscondo, -ere, abscondi, absconditus** – I hide. She seeks to hide the blade, then to 'hide' it in her chest (by suicide).

19 **pectus, -oris (n)** – chest, breast; **quod profecto fecisset** – 'which she would certainly have done'; **timor, -oris (m)** – fear; **timore tanti flagitii** – 'out of fear of such a great crime'.

20 **flagitium, -i (n)** – crime, shameful deed; **temerarius, -a, -um** – reckless; **delabor, delabi, delapsus sum** – I slip; **evolo, -are** – I fly from; **nisi ferrum evolasset** (= *evolavisset*) – 'if the blade had not flown from'; **lassus, -a, -um** – exhausted; **salute defecta** – 'deprived of salvation' (*deficio* has a different meaning from its use in line 17).

21 **saepius** (comparative form of *saepe*) – 'again and again'; **divinus, -a, -um** – divine; **vultus, -us (m)** – face, expression; **intueor, -eri, intuitus sum** – I gaze upon; **pulchritudo, -inis (f)** – beauty; **recreatur animi** – 'she is restored in her soul': note the pun here – Psyche (which means 'soul' in Greek) is said to be 'restored in her soul'.

Apuleius gives a description of the beautiful god, Cupid.

videt capitis aurei genialem caesariem ambrosia temulentam, cervices lacteas genasque purpureas pererrantes crinium globos decoriter impeditos, alios antependulos, alios retropendulos, quorum splendore nimio fulgurante iam et ipsum lumen lucernae vacillabat. per umeros volatilis dei pinnae roscidae micanti flore candicant et quamvis alis quiescentibus extimae plumulae tenellae ac delicatae tremule resultantes inquieta lasciviunt. ceterum corpus glabellum atque luculentum et quale peperisse Venerem non paeniteret. ante lectuli pedes iacebat arcus et pharetra et sagittae, magni dei propitia tela.

25

30

(*Metamorphoses* V.22.5–7)

Names and places
Venus, Veneris (f): Venus, goddess of love.

Q. How does Apuleius depict the beauty of Cupid?

Q. What do you notice about the order in which Apuleius describes Cupid's body?

Q. Explain what Apuleius means by saying that Venus had no regrets at giving birth to Cupid (line 30).

Q. Why do you think Apuleius gives such a lengthy description of Cupid at this point in the story?

GCSE vocabulary: *ac, alii ... alii, atque, caput, corpus, deus, iaceo, iam, ipse, magnus, per, pes, qualis, -que, qui, video.*

23 **aureus, -a, -um** – golden; **genialis, -e** – delightful (or: rich, abundant); **caesaries, -ei (f)** – hair; **ambrosia, -ae (f)** – ambrosia (a food of the gods); **temulentus, -a, -um** – drunk; **cervix, -icis (f)** – neck (Apuleius uses the plural form in Latin, but translate it as singular).

24 **lacteus, -a, -um** – milky white; **gena, -ae (f)** – cheek; **purpureus, -a, -um** – rosy; **pererro, -are** – I stray over, I wander; **crinis, -is (m)** – hair (usually plural in Latin); **globus, -i (m)** – tuft (of hair); **decoriter** – gracefully.

25 **impeditus, -a, -um** – bound; **antependulus, -a, -um** – hanging in front; **retropendulus, -a, -um** – hanging behind: both words agree with *globos*; **quorum** – this refers back to the tufts of hair.

26 **splendor, -oris (m)** – brilliance; **nimius, -a, -um** – extreme; **fulguro, -are** – I shine, I flash; **quorum splendore nimio fulgurante** – the ablative *splendore* is being used in a causal sense: 'because of the excessive shining brilliance of them'; **et** – translate here as 'too' or 'even'; **lumen, -inis (n)** – the light; **lucerna, -ae (f)** – lamp; **vacillo, -are** – I flicker: the subject of the verb is *lumen*.

27 **umerus, -i (m)** – shoulder; **volatilis, -e** – flying; **pinna, -ae (f)** – feather; **roscidus, -a, -um** – dewy; **mico, -are** – I quiver, I glisten; **flos, floris (m)** – brightness, bloom; **micanti flore** – 'with glistening brightness'; **candico, -are** – I gleam, I am white: the subject is *pinnae*.

28 **quamvis** – although; **ala, -ae (f)** – wing; **quiesco, -ere** – I am at rest; **alis quiescentibus** – an ablative absolute phrase to be taken with *quamvis*: 'although his wings were at rest'; **extimus, -a, -um** – at the edge (to be taken with *plumulae*); **plumula, -ae (f)** – little feather; **tenellus, -a, -um** – tender, soft; **delicatus, -a, -um** – delicate.

29 **tremulus, -a, -um** – trembling, rippling (*tremule* is an adverb); **resulto, -are** – I quiver; **inquietus, -a, -um** – restless: *inquieta* is neuter plural and is being used as an adverb here; **lascivio, -ere** – I play; **tremule resultantes inquieta lasciviunt** – '(the little feathers) rippling and quivering played restlessly'; **ceterus, -a, -um** – the rest of; **glabellus, -a, -um** – smooth (supply *erat*).

30 **luculentus, -a, -um** – shining; **pario, parere, peperi, partus** – I give birth to; **paenitet, paenituit** (+ accusative) – it is a source of regret to; **et quale peperisse Venerem non paeniteret** – 'and such that Venus did not regret having given birth to' (*paeniteret* is a characteristic or generic subjunctive); **ante** – in front of.

31 **lectulus, -i (m)** – bed; **pedes** – plural, but translate as 'the foot'; **arcus, -us (m)** – bow; **pharetra, -ae (f)** – quiver; **sagitta, -ae (f)** – arrow; **propitius, -a, -um** – gracious.

32 **telum, -i (n)** – weapon.

Psyche pricks her finger with one of Cupid's arrows. She falls in love with him.

quae dum insatiabili animo Psyche, satis et curiosa, rimatur atque pertrectat et mariti sui miratur arma, depromit unam de pharetra sagittam et punctu pollicis extremam aciem periclitabunda trementis etiam nunc articuli nisu fortiore pupugit altius, ut per summam cutem roraverint parvulae sanguinis rosei guttae. sic ignara Psyche sponte in Amoris incidit amorem. tunc magis magisque cupidine flagrans Cupidinis, prona in eum efflictim inhians, patulis ac petulantibus saviis festinanter ingestis, de somni mensura metuebat. 35

40

(*Metamorphoses* V.23.1–3)

Names and places
Psyche, Psyches (f): Psyche.

Cupido, Cupidinis (m): Cupid.

Amor, Amoris (m): Love (representing Cupid).

Q. Apuleius uses an oxymoron by saying that Psyche fell in love with Cupid 'in ignorance' (*ignara*) and 'of her own free will' (*sponte*): explain this oxymoron.

Q. *Psyche in Amoris incidit amorem*, and *cupidine flagrans Cupidinis* (lines 37–9): explain the puns Apuleius uses.

Q. What does Apuleius mean by saying that Psyche 'was afraid about the length of his sleep'? (line 40)

GCSE vocabulary: *ac, altus, amor, animus, arma, atque, de, dum, etiam, fortis, is, maritus, miror, nunc, per, qui, sanguis, sic, summus, suus, ut.*

33 **quae** – this refers back to the weapons (*tela*) of Cupid: translate as 'these'. **insatiabilis, -e** – insatiable: in *Phaedrus* 252a-b, the philosopher Plato discusses how the soul always seeks to look upon the essence of beauty, and that such contemplation gives wings to the soul as it looks upon even physical beauty, much as Psyche contemplates Cupid here; **satis** – here: 'very'; **curiosus, -a, -um** – curious; **satis et curiosa** – 'and very curious as well'; **rimor, -ari** – I examine.

34 **pertrecto, -are** – I handle; **depromo, -ere** – I take out; **pharetra, -ae (f)** – quiver.

35 **sagitta, -ae (f)** – arrow; **punctus, -us (m)** – pricking, prick; **pollex, pollicis (m)** – thumb; **punctu pollicis** – 'by pricking her thumb'; **extremus, -a, -um** – furthest; **acies, -ei (f)** – point, edge: Psyche has touched the tip of the arrow; **periclitabundus, -a, -um** – testing; **tremens, trementis** – trembling: *trementis* agrees with *articuli*.

36 **articulus, -i (m)** – finger; **nisus, -us (m)** – a push; **pungo, -ere, pupugi, punctus** – I prick; **altius** – too deeply; **cutis, cutis (f)** – skin; **per summam cutem** – 'over the surface of her skin'.

37 **roro, -are** – I moisten, I drip; *roraverint* is perfect subjunctive as it is in a result clause; **parvulus, -a, -um** – tiny; **roseus, -a, -um** – rosy; **gutta, -ae (f)** – drop; **ignarus, -a, -um** – without realizing, in ignorance.

38 **sponte** – of her own accord; **incido, -ere, incidi, incasus** – I fall in; **tunc** – then; **magis magisque** – more and more; **cupido, cupidinis (f)** – desire.

39 **flagro, -are** – I burn; **pronus, -a, -um** – leaning forward; **prona in eum** – 'leaning over him'; **efflictim** – desperately; **inhio, -are** – I gape; **patulus, -a, -um** – open-mouthed.

40 **petulans, petulantis** – sensuous, playful; **savium, -i (n)** – kiss; **festinanter** – quickly; **ingero, -ere, ingessi, ingestus** – I put upon; **saviis ingestis** – an ablative absolute, literally: 'with kisses having been put upon (him)'; **somnus, -i (m)** – sleep; **mensura, -ae (f)** – length; **metuo, -ere** – I fear.

Hot oil from the lamp falls on Cupid, who then flies away from Psyche.

sed dum bono tanto percita saucia mente fluctuat, lucerna illa sive perfidia pessima sive invidia noxia sive quod tale corpus contingere et quasi basiare et ipsa gestiebat, evomuit de summa luminis sui stillam ferventis olei super umerum dei dexterum. hem audax et temeraria lucerna et amoris vile ministerium, ipsum ignis totius deum aduris, cum te scilicet amator aliquis, ut diutius cupitis etiam nocte potiretur, primus invenerit. sic inustus exsiluit deus visaque detectae fidei colluvie prorsus ex osculis et manibus infelicissimae coniugis tacitus avolavit. 45

(*Metamorphoses* V.23.4–6)

The narrator
It is worth remembering that the story of Cupid and Psyche is a story within the larger story of the adventures of Lucius. Lucius, changed into the form of an ass, was imprisoned in a cave with a young girl. An old woman told her the story of Cupid and Psyche to comfort her in her distress.

Inventions
It was common in the ancient world to believe that all objects had been invented by a specific individual. Here, Apuleius claims that some lover invented the lamplight so that lovers could enjoy themselves even at night-time when it was dark.

Q. In what ways does Apuleius personify the lamp?
Q. How do you think Psyche felt at the end of this scene?
Q. What emotions do you think Cupid experienced?

GCSE vocabulary: *amor, audax, bonus, corpus, cum, de, deus, diu, dum, etiam, ex, infelix, ille, invenio, ipse, manus, nox, primus, quod, sed, sic, summus, talis, tantus, totus, tu, ut, video.*

41 **percitus, -a, -um** – roused; **saucius, -a, -um** – wounded; *saucia* is nominative (agreeing with Psyche) and *mente* is ablative: 'wounded in her mind'; **fluctuo, -are** – I am agitated; **lucerna, -ae (f)** – lamp.

42 **sive … sive … sive …** – whether … or … or; **perfidia, -ae (f)** – treachery; **pessimus, -a, -um** – most wicked; **invidia, -ae (f)** – envy; **noxius, -a, -um** – harmful; **sive perfidia pessima sive invidia noxia** – causal ablative phrases: 'whether because of … or because of …'; **sive quod** – 'or because': the change from causal ablative to a clause with *quod* gives greater emphasis to the last of the tricolon* of reasons; **contingo, -ere** – I touch.

43 **quasi** – 'as it were'; **basio, -are** – I kiss; **et ipsa** – 'it too' (i.e. the lamp); **gestio, -ire** – I long (to do something): this verb governs the two infinitives *contingere* and *basiare*; **evomo, -ere, evomui** – I spew out; **de summa luminis sui** – 'from the top of its light' (i.e. the spout or opening at the top of the lamp).

44 **stilla, -ae (f)** – a drop; **ferveo, fervere** – I boil, I am hot; **oleum, -i (n)** – oil; **super** – on; **umerus, -i (m)** – shoulder; **dexter, dextera, dexterum** – right; **hem** (an exclamation expressing shock and anger) – oh! what!: we are to understand the narrator (the old woman in the cave) addressing the lamp here.

45 **temerarius, -a, -um** – reckless; **lucerna, -ae (f)** – lamp; **vilis, -e** – worthless; **ministerium, -i (n)** – assistant; **ignis, -is (m)** – fire; **totius** – genitive singular of *totus* agreeing with *ignis*.

46 **aduro, -ere** – I burn; **cum** – even though (take this with the subjunctive verb *invenerit*); **scilicet** – of course, as everyone knows; **amator, -oris (m)** – lover; **aliquis** – some; **diutius** – for even longer; **cupitum, -i (n)** – desire.

47 **nocte**; (ablative) – 'at night'; **potior, potiri** – I enjoy: *potiretur* is subjunctive as it is a purpose clause – nouns following this verb take the ablative case, which here is *cupitis*; **invenerit** – 'invented'; **inuro, -ere, inussi, inustus** – I burn, I scorch; **exsilio, -ire, exsilui** – I leap up.

48 **detego, -ere, detexi, detectus** – I betray, I uncover; **fides, fidei (f)** – trust, confidence; **colluvies, -ei (f)** – filth; **visaque detectae fidei colluvie** – *visa colluvie* is an ablative absolute enclosing a genitive phrase, *detectae fidei*: literally 'with the filth of his betrayed trust having been seen'. The idea is that Cupid placed his confidence in Psyche, trusting that she would not look upon him. Psyche has now betrayed that trust, and has thus made it (the trust) filthy to look upon; **prorsus** – straightaway; **osculum, -i (n)** – kiss.

49 **coniunx, coniugis (f)** – wife; **tacitus, -a, -um** – in silence; **avolo, -are** – I fly away.

As Cupid flies away, Psyche grabs his leg and is carried off a short distance before falling to the ground tired. Cupid then addresses Psyche.

at Psyche, statim resurgentis eius crure dextero manibus ambabus 50
adrepto, sublimis evectionis adpendix miseranda et per nubilas
plagas penduli comitatus extrema consequia, tandem fessa delabitur
solo. nec deus amator humi iacentem deserens, involavit proximam
cupressum, deque eius alto cacumine sic eam graviter commotus
adfatur: 'ego quidem, simplicissima Psyche, parentis meae Veneris 55
praeceptorum immemor, quae te miseri extremique hominis
devinctam cupidine infimo matrimonio addici iusserat, ipse potius
amator advolavi tibi.'

(*Metamorphoses* V.24.1–3)

Names and places
Cupido, Cupidinis (m): Cupid.

Psyche, Psyches (f): Psyche.

Venus, Veneris (f): Venus.

Plato, *Phaedrus*
Plato was a Greek philosopher who thought that our physical world was a shadowy copy of the real world, which was a world of intellectual ideas. These ideas were the immaterial templates on which the material world was modelled. Plato encouraged his readers to rise upwards intellectually to contemplate such truth, but warned that the soul sometimes 'fails to see, and through some mischance is filled with forgetfulness and evil and grows heavy, and when it has grown heavy, loses its wings and falls to the earth' (Plato, *Phaedrus* 243c).

simplicissima Psyche
The adjective *simplex* is a recurring epithet or adjective used to describe Psyche. It can be translated as 'simple', and conveys the idea that Psyche is naïve, innocent, without deceit. To what extent do you think Psyche is innocent and a victim of circumstances rather than being the agent of her own downfall?

Q. What impression do you have of Psyche at this point?

Q. How do you think Cupid was feeling?

Q. Do you think the description of Psyche here is similar to what Plato says in the *Phaedrus* quotation above?

GCSE vocabulary: *altus, de, deus, ego, gravis, homo, iaceo, ipse, is, iubeo, manus, meus, miser, per, proximus, qui, sic, statim, surgo, tandem, tu.*

50   at – but; resurgo, -ere – I rise up; crus, cruris (n) – leg; dexter, dextera, dexterum – right; ambo, ambae, ambo – both.

51   adripio, -ere, adripui, adreptus – I seize; crure dextero adrepto – this is an ablative absolute; sublimis, -e – soaring, uplifted; evectio, -onis (f) – flight; adpendix, -icis (f) – attachment, appendage: take this as referring to Psyche 'as an attachment to his soaring flight' (*sublimis evectionis*); miseror, -ari – I pity: *miseranda* is a gerundive and can be translated as 'pitiable'; nubilus, -a, -um – cloudy.

52   plaga, -ae (f) – region; pendulus, -a, -um – dangling, trailing; comitatus, -us (m) – escort, companionship; extremus, -a, -um – furthest; consequia, -ae (f) – rear-guard; per nubilas plagas penduli comitatus extrema consequia – *extrema consequia* is nominative and refers to Psyche, with *penduli comitatus* in the genitive: translate as Psyche being 'the furthest rear-guard of the escort trailing through the cloudy regions'. It is an elaborate phrase, and we are to imagine Psyche almost as being at the very back of a military escort for Cupid, as she clings to him and is being trailed through the cloudy sky; fessus, -a, -um – exhausted; delabor, delabi – I fall down.

53   solum, -i (n) – ground; solo – 'on the ground'; nec – and not; amator, -oris (m) – lover; deus amator – 'the god, her lover', could also be translated as 'the god who loved her'; humus, -i (f) – ground (*humi* is the locative and means 'on the ground'); iacentem – the present participle is the object of *deserens*: understand a word such as *eam* (her i.e. Psyche) agreeing with *iacentem*; desero, -ere – I abandon; involo, -are – I fly into (the object is *cupressum*).

54   cupressus, -i (f) – a cypress tree; eius – its (i.e. the cypress tree's); cacumen, -inis (n) – top; commoveo, -ere, -movi, -motus – I agitate.

55   adfor, adfari, adfatus – I address, I speak to (the object is *eam*); quidem – indeed; simplex, simplicis – simple, naïve, innocent; parens, parentis (f) – mother, parent.

56   praeceptum, -i (n) – order, instruction; immemor, immemoris – forgetful of + genitive (followed by *praeceptorum*); extremus, -a, -um – most worthless, lowest, meanest.

57   devincio, -ire, devinxi, devinctus – I bind, I captivate; cupidine – 'by desire (for a wretched and most worthless man)'; infimus, -a, -um – vilest, lowest; matrimonium, -i (n) – marriage; addico, -ere, -dixi, -dictus – I give to, I deliver; potius – rather.

58   amator – 'as a lover'; advolo, -are – I fly to.

Cupid finishes his speech, and then abandons Psyche.

'sed hoc feci leviter, scio, et praeclarus ille sagittarius ipse me telo meo percussi teque coniugem meam feci, ut bestia scilicet tibi viderer et ferro caput excideres meum, quod istos amatores tuos oculos gerit. haec tibi identidem semper cavenda censebam, haec benivole remonebam. sed illae quidem consiliatrices egregiae tuae tam perniciosi magisterii dabunt actutum mihi poenas; te vero tantum fuga mea punivero.' et cum termino sermonis pinnis in altum se proripuit. 60 / 65

(*Metamorphoses* V.24.4–5)

Q. Cupid describes himself as *praeclarus ille sagittarius*: 'that famous archer'. What tone do you think he is using?

Q. Cupid warns Psyche that her 'outstanding advisers' will be punished. Who are these excellent advisers? What tone does Cupid use when referring to them?

GCSE vocabulary: *altus, caput, cum, ego, facio, gero, hic, ille, ipse, meus, poenas do, punio, -que, scio, se, sed, semper, tam, tu, ut.*

59 **leviter** – recklessly, thoughtlessly; **praeclarus, -a, -um** – famous; **sagittarius, -i (m)** – archer; **telum, -i (n)** – weapon.

60 **percutio, -ere, percussi** – I pierce, I wound; **coniunx, coniugis (f)** – wife; **ut viderer** – a result clause: 'with the result that I appeared ...'; **bestia, -ae (f)** – beast; **scilicet** – 'as you know'.

61 **ferrum, -i (n)** – blade, sword; **excido, -ere** – I cut off; **excideres** is to be taken with *ut*: '...you would cut off'; **quod** – the relative pronoun refers back to *caput*; **iste, ista, istud** – that; **oculus, -i (m)** – eye; **amator, -oris (m)** – lover; **gerit** – bears; **istos amatores tuos oculos** – literally 'those eyes, your lovers': translate as 'those eyes which love you'.

62 **haec** – neuter plural of *hic*: 'these things'; **identidem** – repeatedly; **caveo, -ere** – I am on my guard against; **censeo, -ere** – I advise; **haec tibi cavenda censebam** – *cavenda* is a gerundive expressing an obligation, and *tibi* is the dative agent: 'I was advising you to be on your guard against these things'; **benivolus, -a, -um** – kind; **benivole** – kindly: translate as 'out of kindness'.

63 **remoneo, -ere** – I repeatedly warn; **quidem** – indeed; **consiliatrix, -icis (f)** – advisor; **egregius, -a, -um** – outstanding; **illae ... tuae** – 'those ... of yours'.

64 **perniciosus, -a, -um** – destructive, harmful; **magisterium, -i (n)** – instruction, teaching; **actutum** – at once; **poenas** – this is followed by *perniciosi magisterii* which is genitive but is best translated as 'the penalty for their destructive instruction'; **te** – this is the object of the verb *punivero*; **vero** – but; **tantum** – only.

65 **fuga, -ae (f)** – flight; **punivero** – this is the future perfect tense (literally: 'I will have punished'), but can just be translated as future tense here; **terminus, -i (m)** – the end; **sermo, -onis (m)** – speech; **pinna, -ae (f)** – wing; **proripio, -ere, proripui** – I snatch away, I hurry off, I launch; **in altum se proripuit** – literally 'he snatched himself off on high': it could be translated as 'he launched himself into the sky'.

Abandoned, Psyche attempts to take her own life but is rescued by the river.

Psyche vero, humi prostrata et, quantum visu poterat, volatus mariti
prospiciens, extremis affligebat lamentationibus animum. sed ubi
remigio plumae raptum maritum proceritas spatii fecerat alienum,
per proximi fluminis marginem praecipitem sese dedit. sed mitis   70
fluvius, in honorem dei scilicet, qui et ipsas aquas urere consuevit,
metuens sibi, confestim eam innoxio volumine super ripam florentem
herbis exposuit.

(*Metamorphoses* V.25.1–2)

Names and places
Psyche, Psyches (f): Psyche.

Rivers of love
In ancient literature, rivers were often associated with love and lovers. The Roman poet Ovid tells us that even the rivers know what love was, and were accustomed to help young lovers. In *Amores* 3.6, Ovid says that the icy waters of the river Inachus became warm when the river fell in love. In one version of the story of Pyramus and Thisbe, the two lovers were turned into rivers after their deaths.

> Q. Why do you think the river saved Psyche from drowning?
>
> Q. What do you think Apuleius means by saying that Cupid was accustomed to scorch even rivers?
>
> Q. In your opinion, for what reason was the river afraid for himself?

GCSE vocabulary: *animus, aqua, deus, do, facio, flumen, ipse, is, maritus, per, pono, possum, proximus, quantus, qui, rapio, se, sed, ubi.*

Psyche's meeting with Pan
In lines not included in this selection, Psyche now met with Pan who was sitting on the riverbank with the nymph, Echo. Pan was the god of the countryside, of shepherds, and of nature. He was often depicted with half the body of a human, and half of a goat. Recognizing from Psyche's paleness that she was lovesick, Pan urged her not to endanger her life again. Rather, he told her to pray to the god Cupid and seek his favour for her problems.

67 **vero** – however; **humi** – on the ground (locative); **prosterno, -ere, prostravi, prostratus** – I throw myself down; **visus, -us (m)** – sight; **quantum visu poterat** – literally 'as much as she was able with sight': translate to 'as far as she could see'; **volatus, -us (m)** – flight (poetic plural here).

68 **prospicio, -ere** – I look, I watch; **extremus, -a, -um** – utmost; **affligo, -ere** – I distress, I torment; **lamentatio, -onis (f)** – weeping, lamentation.

69 **remigium, -i (n)** – oarage (rowing equipment); **pluma, -ae (f)** – feather (here best translated as 'wing'); **proceritas, -atis (f)** – length; **spatium, -i (n)** – space, distance; **alienus, -a, -um** – foreign, not related, distant; **sed ubi remigio plumae raptum maritum proceritas spatii fecerat alienum** – literally 'but when the length of space had made distant her husband who had been seized on the oarage of his wing', but best translated as: 'but when a lengthy distance had taken her husband from her as he soared on the oars of his wings'. Apuleius is using oars as a metaphor* to represent Cupid flying on his wings.

70 **margo, -inis (f)** – edge, bank; **per marginem** – over the bank; **praeceps, praecipitis** – headlong; **praecipitem sese dedit** – literally 'she gave herself headlong', but translate as 'she flung herself'; **mitis, -e** – gentle.

71 **fluvius, -i (m)** – river; **honor, -oris (m)** – honour; **scilicet qui** – 'who, as we know, . . .'; **et** – translate here as 'even'; **uro, -ere** – I burn; **consuesco, -ere, consuevi** – I am accustomed to.

72 **metuo, metuere** + dative (here *sibi*) – I fear for; **confestim** – immediately; **eam** – the object of the verb *exposuit*; **innoxius, -a, -um** – harmless; **volumen, -inis (n)** – current (of a river); **super** + accusative – on; **ripa, -ae (f)** – riverbank; **floreo, -ere** – I bloom, I abound in; **herba, -ae (f)** – grass; **ripam florentem herbis** – 'riverbank abounding in grass', translate as 'riverbank with abundant grass'.

73 **expono, -ere, exposui** – I put down (the subject is *fluvius*, the object is *eam*).

After being encouraged by the god Pan, Psyche travels on and arrives at the city where her sister lives.

sic locuto deo pastore nulloque sermone reddito sed adorato tantum
numine salutari, Psyche pergit ire. sed cum aliquam multum viae   75
laboranti vestigio pererrasset, inscia* quodam tramite iam die labente
accedit quandam civitatem, in qua regnum maritus unius sororis eius
optinebat. qua re cognita Psyche nuntiari praesentiam suam sorori
desiderat. mox inducta, mutuis amplexibus alternae salutationis
expletis, percontanti causas adventus sui sic incipit: 80

(*Metamorphoses* V.26.1–2)

* NB: some editions print *inscio* here.

> Q. Why do you think Psyche did not reply to the god Pan?
> Q. What range of emotions do you imagine Psyche was experiencing in this passage?

GCSE vocabulary: *cognosco, cum, deus, dies, duco, eo (ire), iam, is, laboro, loquor, maritus, mox, multus, nullus, nuntio, -que, qui, quidam, reddo, regnum, res, sed, sic, suus, unus, via.*

74 **pastor, -oris (m)** – shepherd (the shepherd god is Pan); **sermo, -onis (m)** – speech; **adoro, -are** – I adore; **tantum** – only.

75 **numen, numinis (n)** – (divine) power; **salutaris, -e** – saving; **locuto deo pastore | nulloque sermone reddito | sed adorato tantum numine salutari** – there are three ablative absolute clauses in this sentence: the first refers to the action of Pan, the other two to Psyche's actions; Pan's power is called 'saving' in a general way due to his divine abilities, but specifically in the sense that he has saved Psyche by giving her encouragement; **pergo, -ere** – I proceed, I continue; **aliquam multum viae** – 'a considerable distance on her way' (*aliquam* is an adverb with *multum* followed by the partitive genitive *viae*: literally, 'considerably much of the way').

76 **laboro, -are** – I toil, I labour; **vestigium, -i (n)** – step; **laboranti vestigio** – 'with labouring steps'; **pererro, -are** – I wander over; **inscius, -a, -um** – without realizing (the adjective *inscia* refers to Psyche); **quodam** – ablative singular of *quidam* and agreeing with *tramite*; **trames, tramitis (m)** – path; **die labente** – ablative absolute; **labor, labi** – I fall, wane, fade.

77 **accedo, -ere** – I come to; **quandam** – accusative singular of *quidam* and agreeing with *civitatem*; **civitas, -atis (f)** – city; **unius** – genitive singular of *unus* and agreeing with *sororis*; **soror, -oris (f)** – sister; **eius** – her.

78 **optineo, -ere** – I hold, I maintain; **regnum optinebat** – the husband 'was holding power'; **qua re cognita** – ablative absolute (*qua* is a connecting relative pronoun); **nuntiari** – present passive infinitive; **praesentia, -ae (f)** – presence.

79 **desidero, -are** – I want, I desire; **induco, -ere, induxi, inductus** – I lead in, I usher in (compound verb from *in* + *duco*); **inducta** – understand *ea* (she/Psyche), *(ea) inducta* being ablative absolute; **mutuus, -a, -um** – mutual; **amplexus, -us (m)** – embrace; **alternus, a, -um** – reciprocal, mutual; **salutatio, -onis (f)** – greeting;

80 **expleo, -ere, explevi, expletus** – I complete, I finish; **mutuis amplexibus alternae salutationis expletis** – *mutuis amplexibus expletis* is an ablative absolute, and *alternae salutationis* is genitive: the literal meaning is 'with the mutual embraces of a reciprocal greeting having been completed', better translated as 'when they had finished exchanging mutual embraces and greetings': as usual, Apuleius' style is florid; **percontor, -ari** – I ask, I enquire about; **percontanti** – dative singular of the present participle; understand the dative *ei* with it ('to her', i.e. the sister, 'asking about'): it is dative since it follows *incipit*; **causa, -ae (f)** – reason; **adventus, -us (m)** – coming, arrival; **incipio, -ere** – I begin; **sic incipit** – translate as 'Psyche began to speak as follows' or simply 'Psyche replied as follows'.

Psyche explains to her sister what happened when she tried to kill Cupid.

'meministi consilium vestrum scilicet quo mihi suasistis ut bestiam, quae mariti mentito nomine mecum quiescebat, priusquam ingluvie voraci me misellam hauriret, ancipiti novacula peremerem. sed cum primum, ut aeque placuerat, conscio lumine vultus eius aspexi, video mirum divinumque prorsus spectaculum, ipsum illum deae Veneris   85
filium, ipsum inquam Cupidinem, leni quiete sopitum.'

(*Metamorphoses* V.26.3–4)

Names and places
Venus, Veneris (f): Venus.

Cupido, Cupidinis (m): Cupid.

Q. In line 82, why does Psyche say that her husband had the false name of husband?

Q. Why does Apuleius use the present tense verb *video* in line 84, even though Psyche is reporting past events?

Q. Why does Apuleius describe the lamplight as 'conniving' or 'acting in the know' (*conscio lumine*)?

Q. The word *spectaculum* (line 85) could also be used of entertainment such as took place in the amphitheatres. Why does Apuleius choose this word in this context?

GCSE vocabulary: *consilium, cum, dea, ego, filius, ille, ipse, is, maritus, nomen, qui, -que, sed, ut, vester, video.*

81 **memini, meminisse** – I remember: Psyche assumes her sister will remember how the sisters had told Psyche how to murder her husband (the alleged beast) in Book V.20, telling her to return home then with all his riches where they would arrange a human wedding for Psyche; **scilicet** – namely (explaining their plan); **quo** – by which; **suadeo, -ere, suasi** + dative – I persuade; **suasistis mihi . . . ut premerem bestiam** – this is an indirect command; **bestia, -ae (f)** – beast.

82 **quae** – referring back to *bestiam*; **mentior, -iri, mentitus sum** – I lie; **mentito nomine** – 'under the false name'; **mecum** = *cum me*; **quiesco, -ere** – I rest, I sleep; **priusquam** – before (to be taken with *hauriret*); **ingluvies, -ei (f)** – maw, jaws (ablative *ingluvie* agrees with *voraci*).

83 **vorax, voracis** – greedy; **misellus, -a, -um** (diminutive form of *miser*) – wretched, poor, unfortunate; **haurio, -ire** – I swallow up; **priusquam hauriret** – 'before it could swallow up'; **anceps, ancipitis** – two-edged (ablative agreeing with *novacula*); **novacula, -ae (f)** – blade; **peremo, -ere** – I slay, I kill; **peremerem** – 1st person singular imperfect subjunctive because it follows *mihi suasistis ut*.

84 **cum primum** – 'as soon as'; **ut** – 'as' + indicative *placuerat*; **aeque** – equally (i.e. this plan had equally pleased Psyche and the sisters); **placeo, -ere, placui** – I please; **conscius, -a, -um** – conniving, in the know (*conscio* is ablative agreeing with *lumine*); **vultus** – this is the accusative plural, but can be translated in the singular as 'face'; **aspicio, -ere, aspexi** – I look at; **video** – present tense, but can be translated as the perfect tense.

85 **mirum, -a, -um** – wonderful; **divinus, -a, -um** – divine; **prorsus** – utterly; **divinumque prorsus** – 'and utterly divine'; **spectaculum, -i (n)** – spectacle, sight.

86 **inquam** – I say, I mean; **lenis, -e** – gentle; **quies, quietis (f)** – slumber, rest; **leni quiete** is ablative; **sopio, -ire, sopivi, sopitus** – I put to sleep.

Psyche continues her speech to her sister, explaining what happened when she tried to kill her husband.

'ac dum tanti boni spectaculo percita et nimia voluptatis copia turbata fruendi laborarem inopia, casu scilicet pessimo lucerna fervens oleum rebullivit in eius umerum. quo dolore statim somno recussus, ubi me ferro et igni conspexit armatam, "tu quidem" inquit "ob istud tam dirum facinus confestim toro meo divorte, tibique res tuas habeto. ego vero sororem tuam" – et nomen quo tu censeris aiebat – "iam mihi confarreatis nuptiis coniugabo." et statim Zephyro praecipit ultra terminos me domus eius efflaret.' 90

(*Metamorphoses* V.26.5–7)

Names and places
Zephyrus, -i (m): Zephyr (the west wind).

Q. Can you explain the paradox in *copia* and *inopia* (lines 87–8), where Psyche says she experiences an abundance (*copia*) of pleasure but a lack (*inopia*) of enjoyment?

Q. How much of Psyche's report to her sister matches what we are told happened in lines 41–9?

GCSE vocabulary: *ac, bonus, conspicio, dirus, domus, dum, ego, et, iam, is, laboro, meus, nomen, qui, res, statim, tam, tantus, tu, tuus, ubi.*

87 **dum** – 'while': take this with *laborarem* (*dum* + subjunctive to mean 'while' was common in Apuleius' time); **spectaculum, -i (n)** – spectacle, sight; **percio, -ire, -ivi, -itus** – I rouse, I excite; **nimius, -a, -um** – excessive (*nimia* is ablative agreeing with *copia*); **voluptas, -atis (f)** – pleasure, delight; **copia, -ae (f)** – abundance; **turbo, -are** – I trouble, I disturb.

88 **fruor, frui, fructus sum** – I enjoy; **fruendi** – 'enjoyment': a gerund (a noun coming from a verb), to be taken after *inopia*; **laboro, -are** – (here) I suffer from, I am troubled by; **inopia, -ae (f)** – lack; **dum fruendi laborarem inopia** – literally 'while I was suffering from a lack of enjoying', translate as 'while I suffered from an inability to enjoy it'; **casus, -us (m)** – accident, chance; **scilicet** – 'as we know': Psyche is telling this to her sister for the first time, so it makes sense to see *scilicet* as a comment from the author, Apuleius, addressed to the reader who does know what happened; **pessimus, -a, -um** – superlative of *malus* agreeing with *casu*; **lucerna, -ae (f)** – lamp; **ferveo, -ere** – I boil, I am hot; **oleum, -i (n)** – oil.

89 **rebullio, -ire, -ivi** – I spill a drop of, I bubble up: the object is *oleum*; **umerus, -i (m)** – shoulder; **dolor, -oris (m)** – pain; **quo dolore** – 'by which pain/by this pain' (*quo* is a connecting relative); **somnus, -i (m)** – sleep; **recutio, -ere, recussi, recussus** – I rouse from.

90 **ferrum, -i (n)** – blade, iron; **ignis, -is (m)** – fire (*igni* is ablative); **armo, -are** – I arm; **quidem** – indeed; **inquit** – he said; **ob** (+ accusative) – because of; **iste, ista, istud** – that (*istud* agrees with *dirum facinus*).

91 **facinus, -oris (n)** – crime, deed; **confestim** – immediately; **torus, i (m)** – bed; **divorto, -ere** – I leave (+ *toro meo*); **divorte** is an imperative; *divortere* is used of a woman leaving her husband, hence the derivative 'divorce', but can simply be translated as 'leave' here; **tibique res tuas habeto** – a technical phrase used in Roman law when a husband divorces a woman, it literally means 'have your things to yourself' (*habeto* being a future imperative): translate as 'take your things with you'.

92 **vero** – however; **soror, -oris (f)** – sister: *sororem* is the object of *coniugabo*; **censeo, -ere** – I am known; **aio** – I say (*aiebat* = imperfect); **et nomen quo tu censeris aiebat** – a verbose statement literally meaning 'and he said the name by which you are known', it could be translated as 'and he mentioned the name you are called by', or even 'he mentioned your name'.

93 **confarreatae nuptiae, -arum (f pl)** – marriage ceremony: *confarreatio* was a word used to indicate an ancient and solemn Roman marriage ceremony when bread (*far*) was offered in the presence of priests; **coniugo, -are** – I wed, marry; **praecipio, -ere** (+ dative, here *Zephyro*) – I order.

94 **ultra** (+ accusative) – outside of, beyond; **terminus, -i (m)** – boundary; **domus** – house, translate here as 'palace'; **efflo, -are** – I waft, I breathe out; *efflaret* (the object is *me*) is subjunctive as it is part of an indirect command following *praecipit*: we might have expected *ut efflaret* – the omission of *ut* perhaps suggests the speed of Cupid wanting rid of Psyche.

Psyche's sister rushes off to marry Cupid, but meets her death.

necdum sermonem Psyche finierat, et illa vesanae libidinis et invidiae   95
noxiae stimulis agitata, e re concinnato mendacio fallens maritum,
quasi de morte parentum aliquid comperisset, statim navem ascendit
et ad illum scopulum protinus pergit. et quamvis alio flante vento,
caeca spe tamen inhians, 'accipe me,' dicens 'Cupido, dignam te
coniugem, et tu, Zephyre, suscipe dominam,' saltu se maximo   100
praecipitem dedit. nec tamen ad illum locum vel saltem mortua
pervenire potuit. nam per saxa cautium membris iactatis atque
dissipatis et proinde ut merebatur laceratis visceribus suis, alitibus
bestiisque obvium ferens pabulum interiit.

(*Metamorphoses* V.27.1–3)

Names and places
Psyche, Psyches (f): Psyche.

Cupido, Cupidinis (m): Cupid.

Zephyrus, -i (m): Zephyr (the west wind).

- Q. What impression have you formed of the sister's character in this passage?
- Q. What does Apuleius mean by saying in line 99 the sister had a 'blind hope' (*caeca spe*)?
- Q. Why does the sister refer to herself as *dominam* (line 100) when addressing the Zephyr wind?
- Q. Do you agree that the sister 'deserved' her grisly end?

GCSE vocabulary: *accipio, alius, atque, de, do, dico, ego, fero, ille, locus, maritus, morior, mors, nam, navis, per, possum, res, se, spes, statim, suus, tamen, tu.*

95 **necdum** – not yet; **sermo, -onis (m)** – speech; **finio, -ire, -ii** – I finish; **et** – here treat as the word *cum*: 'when'; **illa** refers to the sister; **vesanus, -a, -um** – insane, mad; **libido, -inis (f)** – lust; **invidia, -ae (f)** – jealousy.

96 **noxius, -a, -um** – harmful, destructive; **stimulus, -i (m)** – spur, incentive; **agitato, -are, -avi, -atus** – I drive on; **concinno, -are, -avi, -atus** – I arrange; **e re concinnato** – improvised, concocted; **mendacium, -i (n)** – lie, falsehood; **e re concinnato mendacio** – 'with a concocted lie' or 'with a lie which she made up'; **fallo, -ere** – I deceive.

97 **quasi** – this word explains the lie: 'to the effect that. . .'; **parens, -entis (m/f)** – parent; **aliquid** – something; **comperio, -ire, comperi, compertus** – I find out, I learn; **ascendo, -ere** – I board (a ship).

98 **scopulus, -i (m)** – cliff (this is that cliff from which Zephyr had previously been transporting the sisters to visit Psyche in Cupid's palace); **protinus** – at once; **pergo, -ere** – I proceed, I travel; **quamvis** – although; **flo, -are, -avi, -atus** – I blow; **ventus, -i (m)** – wind; **alio flante vento** – ablative absolute to be taken with *quamvis*: it was the job of the west wind to bring the sisters to the palace.

99 **caecus, -a, -um** – blind (*caeca* is ablative with *spe*); **inhio, -are** – I gape, I look with longing; **caeca spe inhians** – 'yearning with blind hope'; **dignus, -a, -um** (+ ablative) – worthy of (followed by ablative *te*); **dignam** agrees with *coniugem*.

100 **coniunx, coniugis (f)** – wife; **suscipio, -ere** – I receive; **saltus, -us (m)** – leap, jump; **maximus, -a, -um** – superlative of *magnus*.

101 **praeceps, praecipitis** – headlong; **se dedit** – literally 'she gave herself', translate the idiom as 'she threw herself'; **nec vel saltem mortua** – 'not even dead': the point is that she certainly did not reach the bottom of the cliff alive, nor did she even arrive there dead, seeing that her body was so mangled and dismembered on the way down.

102 **pervenio, -ire** – I reach; **saxum, -i (n)** – rock; **cautes, -tis (f)** – craggy rock (*cautium* is genitive plural); **per saxa cautium** – a pleonasm, literally 'through the rocks of craggy rocks', translate as 'from one rock to another'; **membrum, -i (n)** – limb; **iacto, -are, -avi, -atus** – I throw.

103 **dissipo, -are, -avi, -atus** – I scatter; **membris iactatis atque dissipatis** – an ablative absolute; **proinde ut** – just as; **mereor, -eri** – I deserve; **lacero, -are, -avi, -atus** – I tear to pieces, I mutilate; **viscera, -erum (n pl)** – the entrails, the inner parts of the body; **laceratis visceribus suis** – an ablative absolute; **ales, alitis (m/f)** – bird.

104 **bestia, -ae (f)** – wild beast; **obvius, -a, -um** (+ dative) – in the way of: here translate simply as 'for'; **pabulum, -i (n)** – food; **ferens** – present participle, understand the sister as the subject; **intereo, -ire, -ii** – I die (the subject is 'she', the sister).

Psyche continues wandering and reaches the city where her other sister lives. This sister too meets a swift death.

nec vindictae sequentis poena tardavit. nam Psyche rursus errabundo 105
gradu pervenit ad civitatem aliam, in qua pari modo soror morabatur
alia. nec setius et ipsa fallacie germanitatis inducta et in sororis
sceleratas nuptias aemula, festinavit ad scopulum inque simile mortis
exitium cecidit.

(*Metamorphoses* V.27.4–5)

Names and places
Psyche, Psyches (f): Psyche.

Q. How does Apuleius portray the second sister in this passage?
Q. Does this scene again make you judge Psyche in a different way?

GCSE vocabulary: *ad, alius, cado, duco, festino, in, ipsa, modus, mors, nam, poena, qui, -que, sequor.*

105 **nec** – and not; **vindicta, -ae (f)** – vengeance; **sequentis** – literally 'the following', so translate here as 'the second': it agrees with *vindictae*; **tardo, -are, -avi** – I am slow in coming; **nec vindictae sequentis poena tardavit** – 'the punishment of the second vengeance was not slow in coming'; **rursus** – again; **errabundus, -a, -um** – wandering.

106 **gradus, -us (m)** – step (*gradu* agrees with *errabundo*); **pervenio, -ire, perveni** – I reach, I arrive at; **civitas, -atis (f)** – city; **par, paris** – equal; **pari modo** – 'in a similar way': Apuleius seems to imply that the sisters enjoyed a similar lifestyle; **soror, -oris (f)** – sister (*soror* agrees with *alia*); **moror, morari** – I live.

107 **nec setius** – 'not otherwise', so translate as 'likewise' and take it with *inducta*; **et ipsa** – she too; **fallacies, -ei (f)** – trickery, ruse; **germanitas, -atis (f)** – sisterhood; **induco, -ere, induxi, inductus** – I take in, I deceive: *inducta* is a perfect passive participle; **et ipsa fallacie germanitatis inducta** – 'she too, having been taken in by the sisterhood's trickery', translate simply as '. . . by her sister's trickery'.

108 **sceleratus, -a, -um** – wicked; **nuptiae, -arum (f pl)** – marriage; **aemulus, -a, -um** – eager; **in sororis sceleratas nuptias aemula** – literally, 'eager for the wicked marriage of her sister', translate as 'eager to replace her sister in a wicked marriage'; **scopulus, -i (m)** – cliff; **similis, -e** – similar (*simile* agrees with *exitium*).

109 **exitium, -i (n)** – destruction; **cado, -ere, cecidi** – I fall.

Figure 4 *Paris, Musée du Louvre, Cupid and Psyche, 1788, by Antonio Canova (1757–1822), marble sculpture.*
Photo: DEA/G. DAGLI ORTI/Contributor/Getty Images.

What happens next?

After her sisters' deaths, Psyche continued on her wanderings. She came to a temple of the goddess Ceres, and when she saw the disarray inside the temple, she decided to arrange neatly the offerings there. Ceres, the goddess of the harvest, was unable to assist her as she would not oppose another goddess (in this case, Venus).

Venus continued to torture Psyche, even sending Worry and Sadness to afflict her. Venus then gave Psyche three impossible tasks to perform, but by various interventions Psyche managed to complete them all. Firstly, she was shown a mixed pile of seeds, wheat, beans, etc. and told to arrange them into orderly piles. Thankfully, an army of ants took pity on her and completed the task. Secondly, she was told to fetch golden wool from a flock of very dangerous sheep. In despair, Psyche intended to take her own life again, but was instructed by a reed to gather the wool which had come off the sheep and could be gathered from the shrubs nearby. For the third task, she was asked to gather water from the source of the River Styx – Jupiter himself helped her complete this task.

Finally, Venus ordered Psyche to go to the Underworld to gather a dose of the goddess Proserpina's beauty. Psyche despaired and tried to throw herself from a tower, but the tower spoke and advised her how to enter the Underworld. Psyche eventually got the dose of beauty but, before giving it to Venus, her curiosity got the better of her. She opened the box of beauty, intending to increase her own beauty, but instead was sent into a deep sleep.

At this point Cupid, who had recovered from his wounds, flew from Venus' house and saw Psyche asleep on the ground. Cupid then flew off with Psyche, now awakened, in order to give the box to Venus. He appealed to Jupiter to assist him with his case. Jupiter agreed (so long as Cupid agreed to help him in the future) and Venus was warned not to obstruct Cupid and Psyche. Psyche was given ambrosia and made immortal before marrying Cupid. They had a child whom they called Pleasure, the offspring of the union of Cupid (desire) and Psyche (soul).

Final questions

- To what extent do you think Psyche was responsible for her own sufferings?
- Do you find the story of Cupid and Psyche enjoyable and interesting to read?
- Are there any defects in the storyline?
- What opinion do you have of the nature of the gods and goddesses in this story?
- What impact do you think this story would have had upon the listeners in the cave (Lucius and the girl)?

Verse Literature A

2027–28 Prescription

The selection comes from Ovid, *Metamorphoses* IV, lines 55–166. The text is from R. J. Tarrant's 2004 edition of the *Metamorphoses* in the Oxford Classical Text series, with minor changes of punctuation to help the GCSE student.

Ovid

Publius Ovidius Naso was born in central Italy in 43 BCE. His father was wealthy enough to send him to Rome for his education, where he studied rhetoric. He later studied in Athens and travelled in Asia Minor before returning to Rome to begin a political career. Public life, however, did not appeal to him as much as poetry, which he had begun to write at an early age. Writing verse came easily to him, especially the elegiac couplets that were the standard form for love poetry: *quod temptabam dicere versus erat* ('whatever I tried to say was verse', *Tristia* IV.10.26).

Ovid quickly gained a reputation as a poet. Among his early works were the *Heroides* ('Heroines'), imaginary letters from female figures of mythology to their absent husbands and lovers, and the *Amores* ('Loves'), a supposedly autobiographical account of the misadventures of a poet in love. By 8 CE he was the leading poet of his day when he was suddenly banished from Rome by the emperor Augustus.

According to Ovid himself, the reasons for his exile were *carmen et error* ('a poem and an error'). The racy subject matter of his *Ars Amatoria* ('The Art of Love'), with its advice on seduction and lovemaking, perhaps did not fit with the traditional moral virtues that Augustus was keen to re-establish. As for the 'error', nothing certain is known; Ovid may have found himself involved in some sort of scandal within the imperial family. What is certain is that he was sent away from Rome to the town of Tomis on the shores of the Black Sea. Judging from his *Tristia* ('Sorrows'), a series of poems addressed to his wife, and *Epistulae ex Ponto* ('Letters from Pontus'), he was very unhappy there due to its bleakness, miserable climate and remote location. He never returned to Rome and died in Tomis in 17 CE.

Ovid's poetic output was huge and many would argue that he had the greatest influence of any Roman poet on later Western art and literature. Perhaps his greatest work was the *Metamorphoses* ('Transformations'), completed before his exile. Written in the hexameter metre that was the standard form for epic poetry, its fifteen books link a series of myths, each of which includes some sort of supernatural change of shape. These separate tales with a common theme are told with great imagination and not a little humour – what they may lack of the weighty seriousness of Virgil's great epic the *Aeneid*, they gain in originality, wit and inventiveness. Our selection about the tragic love affair of Pyramus and Thisbe comes from Book IV of the *Metamorphoses*.

Reading Latin poetry in the original language is not easy after only a short time of studying Latin, but we hope that the notes and vocabulary will help you to make sense of the Latin, enjoy the story, and appreciate some of the brilliance of the way in which Ovid tells it.

The story so far

At the start of *Metamorphoses* Book IV, most of the women of Thebes are preparing to celebrate a festival to Bacchus. But not Alcithoe, daughter of Minyas, or her sisters. She does not believe that the wild worship of Bacchus should be allowed and she even denies that he is a god. So, while the rest of the Theban women are outside celebrating Bacchic rites, the daughters of Minyas remain indoors. To pass the time as they spin wool, they decide to tell each other stories.

The first sister hesitates. Should she tell the tale of Dercetis of Babylon, who was turned into a fish? Or how Dercetis' daughter grew wings and was turned into a dove? Or the story of a water nymph who changed the bodies of young men into fish, until the same thing happened to her? The tale she chooses is how a mulberry tree that once had white berries began to produce red ones, dyed by the stain of blood: 'this story pleased her; this is the tale she began as she spun her woollen thread' (*Metamorphoses* IV.53–4).

Ovid's story of Pyramus, Thisbe and the mulberry tree is the earliest surviving version of the tale. He seems to have adapted an earlier myth in which Pyramus was changed into a river and Thisbe into a nearby spring (a more dramatic metamorphosis!). A second-century CE mosaic found on Cyprus shows this older version of the myth (see Figure 5 below). Wall paintings from Pompeii, preserved when the city was destroyed by the eruption of Vesuvius in 79 CE, all show Ovid's version of the story.

It is possible that Ovid alludes to the earlier myth through his use of language relating to water (not least, the water-pipe simile). To explore this further, teachers might like to read the following short article (available from JSTOR): Robert Shorrock, 'Ovidian Plumbing in *Metamorphoses* 4', *The Classical Quarterly*, vol. 53, no. 2, 2003, pp. 624–7.

Figure 5 *Second-century* CE *mosaic from Paphos, Cyprus (with the names of Thisbe and Pyramus in Greek letters).*
Photo: Pavel Sytilin/Alamy Stock Photo.

Pyramus and Thisbe are in love, but their parents do not allow them to marry.

Pyramus et Thisbe, iuvenum pulcherrimus alter,
altera, quas Oriens habuit, praelata puellis,
contiguas tenuere domos, ubi dicitur altam
coctilibus muris cinxisse Semiramis urbem.
notitiam primosque gradus vicinia fecit;   5
tempore crevit amor. taedae quoque iure coissent,
sed vetuere patres; quod non potuere vetare,
ex aequo captis ardebant mentibus ambo.
conscius omnis abest; nutu signisque loquuntur,
quoque magis tegitur, tectus magis aestuat ignis.   10

(*Metamorphoses* IV.55–64)

Names and places
Pyramus, -i (m): Pyramus.

Thisbe, -es (f): Thisbe (note that she has a Greek genitive form in *-es*).

Oriens, -entis (m): the East.

Semiramis, -is (f): Semiramis, a queen of Babylon.

Semiramis
By naming Semiramis here, Ovid locates his story in ancient Babylon (about 60 miles south of modern Baghdad in Iraq). According to the Greek historian Herodotus, it was Queen Semiramis who founded Babylon and built huge embankments to protect the city from being flooded by the river Euphrates.

Babylon
The walls of Babylon, made of baked mud-brick, were famously high. Greek and Roman travellers of the time would have been more used to fortifications made of stone.

Q. How well does Ovid set the scene in lines 1–4?
Q. How does Ovid show the growth of the love between Pyramus and Thisbe?
Q. How does he draw attention to the fact that their love was a secret?
Q. What makes line 10 such an effective line?

GCSE vocabulary: *absum, alter, altus, amor, capio, dico, domus, et, facio, habeo, iuvenis, loquor, murus, omnis, pater, possum, primus, puella, pulcher, qui/quae/quod, quoque, sed, sum, tempus, teneo, ubi, urbs.*

1   **alter ... altera** – the one (i.e. Pyramus) ... the other (i.e. Thisbe).

2   **praefero, -ferre, -tuli, -latus** – I prefer; the order is *altera praelata puellis quas Oriens habuit*: literally 'the other, (who was) preferred to (all) the girls which the East had' – Ovid quickly establishes that both lovers were exceptionally beautiful.

3   **contiguus, -a, -um** – touching, i.e. next to each other; **tenuere** (= *tenuerunt*) – they held, i.e. lived in (Ovid likes the alternative perfect tense ending *-ere* for *-erunt*); **ubi** – where; take the word order as *ubi Semiramis dicitur cinxisse altam urbem coctilibus muris*; **altam** – the separation of the adjective *altam* from its noun *urbem* is very common in poetry (hyperbaton*): here the separation and position of *altam* at the start of the phrase draws attention to how high the walls were.

4   **coctilis, -e** – made of baked mud bricks; **cingo, -ere, cinxi** – I surround; **Semiramis** – Semiramis was the queen who founded Babylon; **urbem** – the 'city' is Babylon.

5   **notitia, -ae (f)** – acquaintance, getting to know each other; **gradus, -us (m)** – step; **notitiam primosque gradus** – literally 'their acquaintance and their first steps': translate as 'the first steps of their acquaintance'; **vicinia, -ae (f)** – nearness, i.e. the fact that they lived next door to each other.

6   **cresco, -ere, crevi** – I grow; **taeda, -ae (f)** – marriage torch, i.e. marriage (Ovid assumes that Babylonians had the same Roman custom of torchlit marriage processions); **ius, iuris (n)** – right, law; **taedae iure** – 'in lawful marriage'; **coeo, -ire, -ii** – I come together; *coissent* is pluperfect subjunctive in a past unfulfilled conditional (knowledge not required for the GCSE language paper): 'they would have come together', i.e. if their fathers had not forbidden it.

7   **veto, -are, vetui** – I forbid (*vetuere* = *vetuerunt*, like *tenuere* in line 3); **quod** – 'the thing which'; **potuere** = *potuerunt* (from *possum*).

8   **ex aequo** – equally; take *captis* with *mentibus*: 'after their minds were captured' (i.e. by love); **ardeo, -ere** – I burn (notice the metaphor*); **mens, mentis (f)** – mind; **ambo, ambae, ambo** – both; notice the slow rhythm of this line (see the section on 'Latin Verse Metre' on pp. xiv–xv).

9   **conscius, -a, -um** – aware (i.e. of their secret); **conscius omnis abest** – 'everyone aware was absent' (Ovid means that no one was aware of their secret); **nutus, -us (m)** – nod; **signum, -i (n)** – sign; notice the switch into historic present tenses (*abest, loquuntur, tegitur, aestuat*) – this is a common technique used by writers to make their narrative more vivid as if it is happening in the present. You may translate them as past tenses, as these notes do.

10 **quoque** = *quo* + *que* (not *quoque* = also); **magis** – more; **quoque magis ... (eo) magis** – literally 'and by which the more ... by that much the more', i.e. 'the more ... the more'; **tego, -ere, texi, tectus** – I hide, cover (understand *amor* or *ignis* as the subject of *tegitur*); **aestuo, -are** – I blaze; **ignis, -is (m)** – fire; notice the ABBA word order (chiasmus*) and polyptoton* of *magis tegitur tectus magis*. What do these literary effects emphasize here?

The two lovers communicate through a crack in the wall between their houses.

fissus erat tenui rima, quam duxerat olim
cum fieret, paries domui communis utrique.
id vitium nulli per saecula longa notatum
(quid non sentit amor?) primi vidistis amantes
et vocis fecistis iter, tutaeque per illud   15
murmure blanditiae minimo transire solebant.
saepe, ubi constiterant hinc Thisbe, Pyramus illinc,
inque vices fuerat captatus anhelitus oris,
'invide' dicebant 'paries, quid amantibus obstas?
quantum erat, ut sineres toto nos corpore iungi?   20
aut, hoc si nimium est, vel ad oscula danda pateres!
nec sumus ingrati; tibi nos debere fatemur
quod datus est verbis ad amicas transitus aures.'
talia diversa nequiquam sede locuti
sub noctem dixere 'vale' partique dedere   25
oscula quisque suae non pervenientia contra.

(*Metamorphoses* IV.65–80)

Names and places
Thisbe, -es (f): Thisbe.

Pyramus, -i (m): Pyramus.

Q. What is the effect of the sudden use of the 2nd person plural in lines 14–15 (*vidistis . . . fecistis*)?

Q. What does *toto corpore iungi* suggest about the lovers' feelings for each other (line 20)?

Q. Do you think that Ovid meant *nequiquam* (line 24) to go with *diversa sede* (i.e. the parents' attempts to keep the lovers apart were useless) or *locuti* (i.e. their speaking was useless)?

GCSE vocabulary: *ad, amo, amor, corpus, cum, debeo, dico, do, domus, duco, et, facio, hic/haec/hoc, ille/illa/illud, in, is/ea/id, iter, longus, loquor, nec/neque, nemo, non, nos, nox, olim, per, primus, quantus, qui/quae/quod, quis/quid, saepe, sentio, si, soleo, sub, sum, suus, talis, totus, transeo, tu, ubi, ut, verbum, video, vox.*

11	**findo, -ere, fidi, fissus** – I split (the subject of *fissus erat* is *paries* in the next line); **tenuis, -e** – thin; **rima, -ae (f)** – crack; **duxerat** – literally 'had led' but take here as 'had developed' (the subject is also *paries*).
12	**fio, fieri** – I become (take *cum fieret* as 'when it was being built'); **paries, -etis (m)** – wall; **communis, -e** – shared between (take the datives *domui utrique* after it); **uterque, utraque, utrumque** – each.
13	**vitium, -i (n)** – fault (i.e. the crack); **nulli** (from *nemo*) – 'by no one'; **saeculum, -i (n)** – century, age; **noto, -are, -avi, -atus** – I notice.
14	**quid non sentit amor?** – Ovid means that love notices everything; **vidistis** – the 2nd person plural form shows that Ovid is suddenly addressing the two lovers (apostrophe*); **primi vidistis amantes** – 'you lovers were the first to see'.
15	**vocis iter** – 'a journey of voice', i.e. 'a route for speech'; **tutus, -a, -um** – safe (i.e. undetected by their parents); **illud** – it, i.e. the crack.
16	**murmur, -uris (n)** – whisper (take *murmure* with *minimo*); **blanditiae, -arum (f pl)** – loving words (take the adjective *tutae* with it); **transeo, -ire** – I cross, i.e. pass from one side of the wall to the other.
17	**consisto, -ere, -stiti** – I stand; **hinc** – on this side; **illinc** – on that side; notice the neat chiasmus* of *hinc Thisbe, Pyramus illinc* to show Pyramus and Thisbe next to each other but on opposite sides of the wall.
18	**in vices** – in turn; **capto, -are, -avi, -atus** – I catch, take in (*fuerat captatus* = *captatus erat*); **anhelitus, -us (m)** – breath; **os, oris (n)** – mouth; **anhelitus oris** – 'the breath of their mouth'. The two lovers are inhaling each other's breath through the crack.
19	**invidus, -a, -um** – envious; **invide paries** – vocative case; **paries, -etis (m)** – wall; **quid** – why; **amantibus** – the participle is used as a noun here: 'lovers'; **obsto, -are** (+ dative) – I get in the way of, obstruct.
20	**quantum ... ut sineres ... aut pateres** – 'how much (would it have been) for you to allow us ... or to be open'; **sino, -ere** – I allow; **nos** – accusative case; **iungo, -ere** – I join (*iungi* is the present passive infinitive).
21	**aut** – or; **nimium** – too much; **vel** – at least; **osculum, -i (n)** – kiss; **pateo, -ere** – I am open; **ad oscula danda** – 'for the giving of kisses'.
22	**ingratus, -a, -um** – ungrateful; **fateor, -eri** – I admit, acknowledge (+ accusative and infinitive *nos debere*); **tibi nos debere** – 'that we owe it to you'.
23	**quod** – the fact that; **datus est** – was allowed; **transitus, -us (m)** – passage; **verbis transitus** – 'a passage for words', i.e. a means of communicating; **amicus, -a, -um** – loving (take with *aures*); **auris, -is (f)** – ear.
24	**talia** – such things (object of the participle *locuti*); **diversus, -a, -um** – separated (take *diversa* as agreeing with the ablative *sede*); **sedis, -is (f)** – house; **nequiquam** – in vain, to no avail.
25	**sub noctem** – at nightfall; **dixere** = *dixerunt*; **vale** – farewell, goodbye; **pars, partis (f)** – side: take the dative *parti* with *suae* in the next line and translate as 'to their side of the wall'; **dedere** = *dederunt* (from *do, dare*).
26	**osculum, -i (n)** – kiss; **quisque, quaeque, quidque** – each of them; **pervenio, -ire** – I get through to, reach; **non pervenientia contra** – 'not getting through to the other side'.

Pyramus and Thisbe plan to run away and agree to meet at Ninus' tomb.

postera nocturnos Aurora removerat ignes
solque pruinosas radiis siccaverat herbas:
ad solitum coiere locum. tum murmure parvo
multa prius questi statuunt ut nocte silenti   30
fallere custodes foribusque excedere temptent,
cumque domo exierint, urbis quoque tecta relinquant,
neve sit errandum lato spatiantibus arvo,
conveniant ad busta Nini lateantque sub umbra
arboris; arbor ibi niveis uberrima pomis,   35
ardua morus, erat, gelido contermina fonti.
pacta placent; et lux tarde discedere visa
praecipitatur aquis, et aquis nox exit ab isdem.

(*Metamorphoses* IV.81–92)

Names and places

Aurora, -ae (f): Aurora, the goddess of the dawn.

Ninus, -i (m): Ninus, husband of Queen Semiramis (hence Shakespeare's playful reference to 'Ninny's tomb' in *A Midsummer Night's Dream*) – his tomb perhaps makes an ominous choice for a lovers' meeting-place.

Q. Why do you think Ovid describes the lovers' plan in such detail?
Q. Why is daylight described as being slow to leave?
Q. How effectively does Ovid describe the change from day to night?

GCSE vocabulary: *a/ab, ad, aqua, cum, custos, discedo, domus, et, exeo, ibi, idem, locus, moveo, multus, nox, parvus, -que, quoque, relinquo, soleo, sub, sum, tum, urbs, video, venio.*

27 posterus, -a, -um – next; nocturnus, -a, -um – of the night; removeo, -ere, -movi – I remove; ignis, -is (m) – fire (here a reference to stars).

28 sol, solis (m) – sun; pruinosus, -a, -um – frosty; radius, -i (m) – ray; sicco, -are, -avi – I dry; herba, -ae (f) – grass.

29 solitus, -a, -um – usual; the *solitum locum* is the wall; coeo, -ire, -ii – I meet (*coiere* = *coierunt*); murmur, -uris (n) – whisper.

30 prius – first; queror, queri, questus sum – I complain; multa questi – 'having made many complaints'; statuo, -ere (+ *ut* + subjunctive) – I decide (to do something); silens, -entis – silent.

31 fallo, -ere – I deceive (take as dependent on *temptent*); custos, -odis (m, f) – guard (*custodes* is a reference to their parents who were preventing them meeting); fores, -ium (f pl) – doors; excedo, -ere – I go out; tempto, -are – I try.

32 cumque ... exierint – 'and when they have left'; tectum, -i (n) – building; relinquant, like *temptent*, *conveniant* and *lateant*, is present subjunctive after *statuunt ut* ('they decided to leave ... meet ... and hide').

33 neve – and so that ... not; error, -are – I wander, get lost; latus, -a, -um – wide; spatior, -ari – I walk; arvum, -i (n) – field; lato arvo – 'in open country' (it is common for a preposition like *in* to be omitted in poetry). This is a tricky line: literally 'and so that there might not be (*neve sit*) any getting lost (*errandum*) by them as they walked (*spatiantibus*)', i.e. 'and so that they might not get lost as they walked'.

34 convenio, -ire – I meet; bustum, -i (n) – tomb (take the plural *busta* as singular); lateo, -ere – I hide; umbra, -ae (f) – shade.

35 arbor, -oris (f) – tree (supply *erat* from line 36 with *arbor* – 'there was a tree'); arboris arbor – Ovid is fond of this sort of juxtaposition* (see also line 10); niveus, -a, -um – snow-white; uber, -eris (+ ablative) – fertile with, laden with; pomum, -i (n) – fruit.

36 arduus, -a, -um – high; morus, -i (f) – mulberry tree (remember that the point of including this story in the *Metamorphoses* was to tell how the white fruit of the mulberry tree was changed into red); gelidus, -a, -um – icy, cold; conterminus, -a, -um – next to; fons, fontis (m) – spring (the spring's water is the reason why the lion will come there to drink).

37 pactum, -i (n) – agreement, plan (take the plural *pacta* as singular); placeo, -ere – I am pleasing; pacta placent – 'they liked their plan' (the alliteration* of *p* and the short two-word phrase may suggest the matter-of-fact firmness of their decision); lux, lucis (f) – daylight; tardus, -a, -um – slow; visa – (from *videor*) 'having seemed, seeming'.

38 praecipitor, -ari – I rush headlong; aquis (first time) – 'into the waters'; take the second *aquis* with *ab isdem* ('from the same waters'); *isdem* = *eisdem*; notice the chiastic* balance of *lux praecipitatur aquis ... aquis nox exit*.

Thisbe goes to the meeting-place but has to escape into a cave when she sees a lion. In her haste she drops her cloak, which the lion finds.

callida per tenebras versato cardine Thisbe
egreditur fallitque suos adopertaque vultum   40
pervenit ad tumulum dictaque sub arbore sedit;
audacem faciebat amor. venit ecce recenti
caede leaena boum spumantes oblita rictus
depositura sitim vicini fontis in unda;
quam procul ad lunae radios Babylonia Thisbe   45
vidit et obscurum timido pede fugit in antrum,
dumque fugit, tergo velamina lapsa reliquit.
ut lea saeva sitim multa compescuit unda,
dum redit in silvas, inventos forte sine ipsa
ore cruentato tenues laniavit amictus.   50

(*Metamorphoses* IV.93–104)

Names and places
Thisbe, -es (f): Thisbe.

Babylonius, -a, -um: Babylonian.

> Q. Why do you think Ovid describes Thisbe leaving for the meeting place first?
> Q. How does Ovid create suspense in this passage?
> Q. *sine ipsa* (line 49): why might the lion have been disappointed?

GCSE vocabulary: *ad, amor, audax, dico, dum, ecce, egredior, et, facio, fugio, in, invenio, ipse/ipsa/ipsum, multus, per, pes, qui/quae/quod, redeo, relinquo, saevus, sedeo, silva, sine, sub, suus, ut, venio, video.*

39 **callidus, -a, -um** – clever, skilful: notice the prominent placement of the word at the start of the sentence to draw our attention to it (Thisbe needed to be careful that the door didn't creak); **tenebrae, -arum (f pl)** – darkness (take *per tenebras* with *egreditur* in the next line); **verso, -are, -avi, -atus** – I turn; **cardo, -inis (m)** – hinge.

40 **fallo, -ere** – (here) I escape the notice of; **suos** – her parents; **adoperio, -ire, -ui, adopertus** – I cover; **vultus, -us (m)** – face; **adoperta vultum** – 'covered with respect to her face', i.e. with her face covered.

41 **pervenio, -ire, perveni** – I reach; **tumulus, -i (m)** – mound, tomb; **arbor, -oris (f)** – tree; **dicta sub arbore** – 'under the appointed tree' (where they had agreed to meet).

42 Understand *eam* with **audacem faciebat**; take **ecce** before **venit** (*ecce* often introduces an element of surprise or a dramatic moment); **recens, -entis** – recent, fresh.

43 **caedes, is (f)** – slaughter, blood; **leaena, -ae (f)** – lioness; **boves, boum (m/f pl)** – cattle; **spumo, -are** – I foam; **oblitus, -a, -um** – smeared; **rictus, -us (m)** – jaw; *recenti caede* is dependent on *oblita* ('smeared with the fresh slaughter'); *spumantes rictus* is accusative after *oblita*, i.e. 'with its foaming jaws smeared with . . .'.

44 **depono, -ere, -posui, -positus** – I put aside, quench (*depositura* is a future participle of purpose – 'in order to quench'); **sitis, -is (f)** – thirst (*sitim* is accusative and the object of *depositura*); **vicinus, -a, -um** – nearby; **fons, fontis (m)** – spring; **unda, -ae (f)** – (here) water.

45 **quam** refers to the lioness and is the object of *vidit*: 'Thisbe saw it'; **procul** – from a distance; **luna, -ae (f)** – moon; **radius, -i (m)** – ray; **ad lunae radios** – 'under the rays of the moon'; **Babylonia Thisbe** – the use of the adjective *Babylonia* gives the phrase a rather epic, heroic feel (ironic as Thisbe is about to lose her boldness and hide in a cave!).

46 **obscurus, -a, -um** – dark; **timidus, -a, -um** – fearful; **antrum, -i (n)** – cave; the enclosing word order* of *obscurum timido pede fugit in antrum* perhaps suggests Thisbe sheltering inside the cave.

47 **tergum, -i (n)** – back (take *tergo* with *lapsa* as 'which had slipped from her back'); **velamen, -inis (n)** – veil or cloak (the precise meaning is unclear: perhaps it was the outer cloak which Thisbe took with her to guard against the evening cold); take the plural *velamina* as singular and as the object of *reliquit*; **labor, labi, lapsus sum** – I fall, slip.

48 **ut** (+ indicative) – when; **lea, -ae (f)** – lioness; **sitis, -is (f)** – thirst (*sitim* is accusative); **compesco, -ere, -ui** – I overcome; **unda, -ae (f)** – water.

49 **inventos forte** – 'which it had found by chance' (*inventos* agrees with *amictus*); **sine ipsa** = *sine puella ipsa*.

50 **os, oris (n)** – mouth; **cruentatus, -a, -um** – bloodied; **tenuis, -e** – thin; **lanio, -are, -avi** – I tear at; **amictus, -us (m)** – garment; *tenues amictus*: plural for singular.

When Pyramus reaches the meeting-place he finds a lion's footprints and Thisbe's bloodstained cloak. Thinking that he is responsible for her death, he says farewell to the cloak and plans to kill himself.

serius egressus vestigia vidit in alto
pulvere certa ferae totoque expalluit ore
Pyramus; ut vero vestem quoque sanguine tinctam
repperit, 'una duos' inquit 'nox perdet amantes,
e quibus illa fuit longa dignissima vita, 55
nostra nocens anima est. ego te, miseranda, peremi,
in loca plena metus qui iussi nocte venires
nec prior huc veni. nostrum divellite corpus
et scelerata fero consumite viscera morsu,
o quicumque sub hac habitatis rupe leones! 60
sed timidi est optare necem.' velamina Thisbes
tollit et ad pactae secum fert arboris umbram,
utque dedit notae lacrimas, dedit oscula vesti,
'accipe nunc' inquit 'nostri quoque sanguinis haustus!'
quoque erat accinctus, demisit in ilia ferrum. 65

(*Metamorphoses* IV.105–19)

Names and places
Pyramus, -i (m): Pyramus.

Thisbe, -es (f): Thisbe.

Q. Why do you think Pyramus arrived after Thisbe? How does the word order draw attention to his lateness?

Q. What is effective about the word order of *una duos nox perdet amantes* (line 54)?

Q. How well does Ovid choose his words in line 59?

Q. Do you think Pyramus was right to blame himself for what he thought was Thisbe's death?

GCSE vocabulary: *accipio, ad, altus, amo, corpus, do, duo, e/ex, ego, egredior, et, fero, habito, hic/haec/hoc, ille/illa/illud, in, inquit, iubeo, locus, longus, morior, nec/neque, noster, nox, nunc, -que, qui/quae/quod, quoque, sanguis, sed, sum, sub, te, tollo, totus, traho, unus, ut, venio, video, vita, vulnus.*

51	**serius** – later, too late; **vestigium, -i (n)** – footprint (take *vestigia* with *certa* in the next line); **alto** – *altus* can mean 'deep' as well as 'high'. Pyramus can presumably see the footprints in the moonlight.
52	**pulvis, -eris (m)** – dust; **certus, -a, -um** – clear; **fera, -ae (f)** – wild beast; **expallesco, -ere, -pallui** – I grow pale (a sign of fear); **os, oris (n)** – face.
53	**ut (+ indicative)** – when; **vero** – indeed; **vestis, -is (f)** – cloak; **tingo, -ere, tinxi, tinctus** – I tinge, stain. Notice the delay and enjambment* of Pyramus' name to match his late arrival at the tomb.
54	**reperio, -ire, repperi** – I find; take **una** with **nox** and **duos** with **amantes**; **perdo, -ere** – I destroy (what tense is *perdet*?).
55	**illa** – she (Thisbe); **dignus, -a, -um (+ ablative)** – worthy of.
56	**noster, nostra, nostrum** – our (take here = 'my'); **nocens, -entis** – guilty; **anima, -ae (f)** – soul; the position of *nostra* is emphatic – 'it is my soul which is guilty'; **miserandus, -a, -um** – to be pitied (*miseranda* is vocative: 'you who are to be pitied'); **perimo, -ere, -emi** – I destroy.
57	**loca** – the plural of *locus* (place) often has this neuter form in *-a*; **plenus, -a, -um** – full of; **metus, -us (m)** – fear; the word order is *(ego) qui iussi (ut) venires in loca plena metus*; **iussi** – Pyramus had not actually 'ordered' Thisbe to meet at the tree, but blames himself anyway.
58	**prior, -oris** – first; **huc** – to this place, here; **divello, -ere** – I tear apart (the imperative *divellite* is addressed to the lions of line 60).
59	**sceleratus, -a, -um** – wicked; **ferus, -a, -um** – wild; **consumo, -ere** – I eat; **viscera, -um (n pl)** – guts, insides; **morsus, -us (m)** – bite. This skilfully patterned line has two adjectives separated from two nouns by a verb in the middle: take *scelerata* with *viscera* and *fero* with *morsu*.
60	**quicumque leones** – 'all you lions who . . .'; **leo, -onis (m)** – lion; **rupes, -is (f)** – rock (presumably a rock near where the cave was).
61	**timidus, -a, -um** – fearful; **est timidi** – 'it is the act of a coward'; **opto, -are** – I wish for; **nex, necis (f)** – death; **velamen, -inis (n)** – veil, cloak (*velamina* is plural for singular); **Thisbes** – genitive. The idea is that merely wishing for death isn't enough for Pyramus; he must now carry it out.
62	**pactus, -a, -um** – agreed (the word order is *fert (velamina) secum ad umbram pactae arboris*); **secum** – with him; **arbor, -oris (f)** – tree (where they had agreed to meet); **umbra, -ae (f)** – shade.
63	**ut (+ indicative)** – when; **notus, -a, -um** – well-known (take *notae* with *vesti*); **lacrima, -ae (f)** – tear; **osculum, -i (n)** – kiss; **vestis, -is (f)** – cloak.
64	**accipe** – imperative (as often *accipio* means 'receive' here, not 'accept'); **haustus, -us (m)** – draught, drink (*haustus* is accusative plural and the object of the *accipe*). Notice the *quoque*: Pyramus believes that the cloak has been soaked with Thisbe's blood and so he offers his own blood 'as well'.
65	**quoque** = *quo + -que*; take **quo** with **ferrum** – 'and the sword with which'; **accingo, -ere, accinxi, accinctus** – I equip with (*erat accinctus* = *accinctus erat*); **demitto, -ere, demisi** – I send down, plunge; **ilia, -ium (n pl)** – side, groin; **ferrum, -i (n)** – sword; **demisit in ilia ferrum** – a standard phrase for a fatal wound in the lower body below the rib cage.

Pyramus' blood spurts out like water from a broken pipe and soaks the roots of the mulberry tree. The white berries are now tinged with red.

nec mora; ferventi moriens e vulnere traxit.
ut iacuit resupinus humo, cruor emicat alte,
non aliter quam cum vitiato fistula plumbo
scinditur et tenues* stridente foramine longe*
eiaculatur aquas atque ictibus aera rumpit. 70
arborei fetus aspergine caedis in atram
vertuntur faciem, madefactaque sanguine radix
purpureo tingit pendentia mora colore.

(*Metamorphoses* IV.120–7)
* NB: several editions print *tenui* and *longas* here.

The colour of mulberries
Soaking the roots of a mulberry tree with blood would not make the berries red, of course, but the world of the *Metamorphoses* is a make-believe world in which strange things happen! Mulberries are green or light yellow when unripe, but ripen to a deep red or black colour.

> Q. *nec mora* (line 66): could this be a playful pun on *mora* ('mulberries') in line 73?
>
> Q. Ovid has been criticized for his choice of simile in lines 68–70. How appropriate do you find it?
>
> Q. How is the word order of line 73 effective?

GCSE vocabulary: *ac/atque, altus, aqua, cum, e/ex, et, iaceo, in, longus, morior, nec/neque, non, quam, sanguis, traho, ut, verto, vulnus*.

66 **mora, -ae (f)** – delay; **nec mora (erat)** – there was no delay, straightaway (is it just a coincidence that *mora* occurs eight lines later as 'mulberries'?); **fervens, -entis** – hot, boiling (take *ferventi* as ablative with *vulnere* and understand *ferrum* as the object of *traxit*). Ovid makes Pyramus remove the sword from his wound because the story requires the mulberry tree to be splattered with blood.

67 **ut** – when; *iacuit* is from *iaceo* (I lie down) not *iacio* (I throw); **resupinus, -a, -um** – on his back; **humus, -i (f)** – ground (take *humo* as 'on the ground'); **cruor, -oris (m)** – blood; **emico, -are** – I spurt out (not an exaggeration, as any doctor might confirm).

68 **non aliter quam cum** – 'not otherwise than when', i.e. 'just as when' (it was common in Homeric epic for the death of a hero to be described with a simile*); the word order, interrupted by an ablative absolute, is tricky here – take it as *non aliter cum fistula (vitiato plumbo) scinditur et stridente foramine eiaculatur longe tenues aquas atque rumpit aera ictibus*; **fistula, -ae (f)** – pipe; **vitio, -are, -avi, -atus** – I damage; **plumbum, -i (n)** – lead (the Romans used lead to make pipes); *vitiato plumbo* is ablative: 'when the lead has been damaged' or '(a pipe) with damaged lead'.

69 **scindo, -ere** – I split (the subject of *scinditur* is *fistula*); **tenuis, -e** – thin (take *tenues* as accusative with *aquas*); **strido, -ere** – I hiss (the sound made when water spurts through a hole in a pipe); **foramen, -inis (n)** – hole (take the ablatives *stridente foramine* as 'through the hissing hole'); **longe** – far and wide.

70 **eiaculor, -ari** – I spurt out; **ictus, -us (m)** – impact, beat (the word is used elsewhere of a pulse); **aer, aeris (m)** – air (*aera* is a Greek accusative form); **rumpo, -ere** – I break, break through; Ovid seems to describe the water pumping out in regular jets (like the beating heart of Pyramus?). The simile* from the practical world of Roman plumbing is certainly far removed from the idyllic rural world in which the story is set!

71 **arboreus, -a, -um** – of the tree; **fetus, -us (m)** – fruit (*fetus* is nominative plural here); **aspergo, -inis (f)** – spray; **caedes, -is (f)** – blood; **ater, atra, atrum** – black, dark red.

72 **facies, -ei (f)** – face, but here take as 'colour'; **madefacio, -ere, madefeci, madefactus** – I make wet, drench (take the participle *madefacta* as nominative agreeing with *radix*); **radix, -icis (f)** – root (of the mulberry tree).

73 **purpureus, -a, -um** – purple-red (take *purpureo* with *colore*); **tingo, -ere** – I tinge, stain; **pendo, -ere** – I hang; **morum, -i (n)** – mulberry; **color, -oris (m)** – colour.

Thisbe returns to the tree and finds Pyramus' body.

ecce metu nondum posito, ne fallat amantem,
illa redit iuvenemque oculis animoque requirit, 75
quantaque vitarit narrare pericula gestit.
utque locum et visa cognoscit in arbore formam,
sic facit incertam pomi color; haeret, an haec sit.
dum dubitat, tremebunda videt pulsare cruentum
membra solum retroque pedem tulit oraque buxo 80
pallidiora gerens exhorruit aequoris instar,
quod tremit, exigua cum summum stringitur aura.
sed postquam remorata suos cognovit amores,
percutit indignos claro plangore lacertos
et laniata comas amplexaque corpus amatum 85
vulnera supplevit lacrimis fletumque cruori
miscuit et gelidis in vultibus oscula figens
'Pyrame,' clamavit, 'quis te mihi casus ademit?
Pyrame, responde! tua te, carissime, Thisbe
nominat; exaudi vultusque attolle iacentes!' 90
ad nomen Thisbes, oculos iam morte gravatos
Pyramus erexit visaque recondidit illa.

(*Metamorphoses* IV.128–46)

Names and places
Pyramus, -i (m): Pyramus.

Thisbe, -es (f): Thisbe.

Mourning
Beating one's body and tearing at one's hair were traditional features of mourning (see lines 84–5).

> Q. In line 75, what do you think Ovid means when he says that Thisbe 'looked for the young man with her eyes and mind'?
>
> Q. Do you think *tremebunda* (line 79) is meant to be nominative singular agreeing with Thisbe, or accusative plural agreeing with *membra*? Grammatically and metrically it could be either.
>
> Q. How effective is the simile in lines 81–2?

GCSE vocabulary: *ad, amo, amor, animus, clamo, clarus, cognosco, corpus, cum, dum, ecce, ego, et, facio, fero, gero, hic/haec/hoc, iaceo, iam, ille/illa/illud, in, iuvenis, locus, mors, narro, ne, nomen, periculum, pes, pono, postquam, quantus, qui/quae/quod, quis, redeo, respondeo, sed, sic, sum, summus, suus, tu, tuus, ut, video, vulnus.*

74 **metus, -us (m)** – fear; **nondum** – not yet; **depono, -ere, -posui, -positus** – I lay aside (*metu nondum deposito* is an ablative absolute); **fallo, -ere** – (here) I disappoint; **amantem** – 'her lover', i.e. Pyramus.
75 **oculus, -i (m)** – eye; **requiro, -ere** – I look for.
76 The order is *gestit narrare quanta pericula vitarit*; **gestio, -ire** – I am eager; **vito, -are, -avi** – I avoid (take the perfect subjunctive form *vitarit* as 'she has avoided'). Thisbe can't wait to tell Pyramus about the lion.
77 **ut . . . sic** – although . . . yet; **cognosco, -ere, cognovi** – (here) I recognize; **arbor, -oris (f)** – tree; **forma, -ae (f)** – shape (*formam* is object of *cognovit*).
78 **incertus, -a, -um** – unsure (understand *eam* with *incertam*); **pomum, -i (n)** – fruit; **color, -oris (m)** – colour; **haereo, -ere** – I am unsure; **an haec sit** – 'whether this was it' (i.e. the one they had agreed to meet at). The three monosyllables bring the line to a stumbling, uncertain halt.
79 **dubito, -are** – I hesitate; **tremebundus, -a, -um** – trembling; **pulso, -are** – I beat, strike; **cruentus, -a, -um** – bloody (take *cruentum* with *solum*: 'she saw his limbs beating the bloody ground').
80 **membrum, -i (n)** – limb; **solum, -i (n)** – ground; **retro** – backwards; **os, oris (n)** – face (take the plural *ora* as singular); **buxum, -i (n)** – box-wood (a very pale type of wood); *buxo* is ablative of comparison with *pallidiora*.
81 **pallidus, -a, -um** – pale; **ora gerens** – 'bearing her face'; **exhorresco, -ere, -horrui** – I shudder; **aequor, -oris (n)** – sea; **instar** (+ genitive) – like (take with *aequoris*). Notice the further water imagery and consider the effectiveness of the simile*.
82 **quod** – 'which' (not *quod* = because); **tremo, -ere** – I tremble; **exiguus, -a, -um** – small (*exigua* is ablative with *aura*); **summum** – 'the surface' (of the sea) – nominative here; **stringo, -ere** – I ruffle; **aura, -ae (f)** – breeze.
83 **remoror, -morari, -moratus sum** – I delay (could *remorata* be another pun on *mora* = mulberries?); **suos amores** – plural for singular: 'her lover'.
84 **percutio, -ere** – I strike; **indignus, -a, -um** – unworthy; **clarus, -a, -um** – (here) loud; **plangor, -oris (m)** – blow; **lacertus, -i (m)** – arm.
85 **lanio, -are, -avi, -atus** – I tear; **comae, -arum (f pl)** – hair; **laniata comas** – 'tearing her hair'; **amplector, -i, amplexus sum** – I embrace.
86 **suppleo, -ere, -plevi** – I fill; **lacrima, -ae (f)** – tear; **fletus, -us (m)** – weeping, tears; **cruor, -oris (m)** – blood.
87 **misceo, -ere, -ui** – I mix; **gelidus, -a, -um** – cold; **vultus, -us (m)** – face (take *vultibus* as singular); **osculum, -i (n)** – kiss; **figo, -ere** – I fix, plant. Thisbe finally gets to kiss Pyramus.
88 **casus, -us (m)** – misfortune; **quis . . . casus**: 'what misfortune'; **adimo, -ere, ademi** – I take away; **mihi** – 'from me'.
89 **carus, -a, -um** – dear, beloved (the superlative *carissime* is vocative case).
90 **nomino, -are** – I call; **exaudio** = *audio*; **vultus, -us (m)** – face (plural for singular again); **attolle** = *tolle*; **iacentes** (from *iaceo*)– take as 'drooping'.
91 **ad nomen Thisbes** – 'at the name of Thisbe'; **oculus, -i (m)** – eye; **gravatus, -a, -um** – heavy.
92 **erigo, -ere, erexi** – I raise, open (i.e. eyes); **visa . . . illa** – ablative absolute; **recondo, -ere, -didi** – I close again (understand *oculos*).

Thisbe sees her bloodstained cloak and realizes the truth. She resolves to die.

quae postquam vestemque suam cognovit et ense
vidit ebur vacuum, 'tua te manus' inquit 'amorque
perdidit, infelix. est et mihi fortis in unum   95
hoc manus, est et amor; dabit hic in vulnera vires.
persequar extinctum letique miserrima dicar
causa comesque tui, quique a me morte revelli
heu sola poteras, poteris nec morte revelli.
hoc tamen amborum verbis estote rogati,   100
o multum miseri meus illiusque parentes,
ut quos certus amor, quos hora novissima iunxit,
componi tumulo non invideatis eodem.
at tu, quae ramis arbor miserabile corpus
nunc tegis unius, mox es tectura duorum,   105
signa tene caedis pullosque et luctibus aptos
semper habe fetus, gemini monimenta cruoris.'

(*Metamorphoses* IV.147–61)

> Q. 'Thisbe's words are too clever to be really moving.' Do you agree?

GCSE vocabulary: *ad, amor, cognosco, corpus, dico, do, duo, ego, et, fortis, habeo, hic/haec/hoc, idem, ille/illa/illud, infelix, inquit, manus, meus, miser, mors, mox, multus, nec/neque, non, novus, nunc, possum, postquam, -que, qui/quae/quod, rogo, semper, sequor, solus, sum, suus, tamen, teneo, tu, tuus, unus, ut, verbum, video, vulnus.*

93	**quae postquam** – 'after she . . . ' (i.e. Thisbe); **vestis, -is (f)** – cloak; **ensis, -is (m)** – sword (take the ablative *ense* with *vacuum*: 'empty of its sword'); **vestemque . . . et ebur** – 'both her cloak . . . and the scabbard'.
94	**ebur, -oris (n)** – ivory, i.e. scabbard; **vacuus, -a, -um** – empty.
95	**perdo, -ere, -didi** – I destroy; **est mihi** – 'there is to me', i.e. 'I have'; notice the *et* in lines 95 and 96 – the sense is 'I <u>also</u> have . . . '; **in unum hoc** – 'for this one deed'; **fortis . . . manus** – 'a strong hand': Thisbe summons the courage to end her life.
96	**hic** – i.e. *amor*; **in vulnera** – 'for the wounds' (which Thisbe plans to inflict on herself); **vires, -ium (f pl)** – strength.
97	**persequor, -i** – I follow (take *persequar* as future and understand *te* as the object); **extinctus, -a, -um** – dead; **letum, -i (m)** – death.
98	**causa, -ae (f)** – cause (like Pyramus earlier, Thisbe blames herself for what has happened); **comes, -itis (m/f)** – companion; **quique** – 'and you who'; **a me** – 'from me'; **revello, -ere** – I tear away (*revelli* is a passive infinitive dependent on *poteras*: 'you could have been torn away').
99	**heu** – alas; **sola** – ablative ('by death alone'); **poteris** – future tense; **nec morte** – 'not even by death'. Thisbe's point is that when Pyramus was alive death was the only thing that could have separated them, but now not even death will be able to separate them. Notice the chiasmus* of *revelli poteras, poteris . . . revelli*.
100	**ambo, -ae, -o** – both; **hoc . . . estote rogati** – 'be asked (to do) this' (addressed to the *parentes* in the next line).
101	**multum miseri** = *miserrimi*; **meus illiusque parentes** – 'my parents and his'; **parens, -entis (m, f)** – parent. Notice the mournful alliteration* of <u>m</u>ultum <u>m</u>iseri <u>m</u>eus.
102	**ut** – that (introducing Thisbe's request); the order is *ut non invideatis (eos) quos certus amor (et) hora novissima iunxit componi eodem tumulo*; **quos** – those whom; **certus, -a, -um** – sure, steadfast; **hora, -ae (f)** – hour; **hora novissima** – 'the most recent (= final) hour' i.e. the hour of death; **iungo, -ere, iunxi** – I join together.
103	**compono, -ere** – I place/bury together (*componi* is passive infinitive); **tumulus, -i (m)** – burial mound, tomb (take *tumulo* with *eodem*); **invideo, -ere** – I begrudge, deny; **ut . . . non invideatis** – 'that you do not begrudge', i.e. 'that you allow'; **eodem** is the ablative of *idem* ('the same').
104	**at** – but; **tu** – you, i.e. the tree; **arbor, -oris (f)** – tree (*quae . . . arbor* = *arbor quae*); **ramus, -i (m)** – branch; **miserabilis, -e** – pitiable.
105	**tego, -ere, texi, tectus** – I cover (*tectura* is the future participle); **unius . . . duorum** – genitive, dependent on *corpus*. Thisbe's lament is full of rhetorical effects: notice here the polyptoton* of *tegis . . . tectura* and the double balance of *nunc . . . mox* and *unius . . . duorum*.
106	**signum, -i (n)** – sign; **tene** – imperative of *teneo*; **caedis, -is (f)** – death; **pullus, -a, -um** – dark (take *pullos* with *fetus* in the next line); **luctus, -us (m)** – mourning (*luctibus* is plural for singular); **aptus, -a, -um** (+ dative) – suitable for.
107	**fetus, -us (m)** – fruit (*fetus* is accusative plural); **geminus, -a, -um** – double; **monimentum, -i (n)** – memorial; take the plural *monimenta* as singular; **cruor, -oris (m)** – 'blood' in line 86 but here = 'death'.

Thisbe uses Pyramus' sword to kill herself. Their parents and the gods, in different ways, are touched by their tragic ends.

dixit et aptato pectus mucrone sub imum
incubuit ferro, quod adhuc a caede tepebat.
vota tamen tetigere deos, tetigere parentes; 110
nam color in pomo est, ubi permaturuit, ater,
quodque rogis superest una requiescit in urna.

(*Metamorphoses* IV.162–6)

> Q. What is the effect of the repetition of *tetigere* in line 110?
> Q. *quodque rogis superest una requiescit in urna* (line 112): how does this make an effective end to the story?

GCSE vocabulary: *a/ab, deus, dico, et, in, nam, -que, qui/quae/quod, sub, sum, tamen, ubi, unus.*

108 **apto, -are, -avi, -atus** – I fit (take *aptato* with *mucrone* as an ablative absolute); **pectus, -oris (n)** – chest, breast; **mucro, -onis (m)** – tip (of the sword); **imus, -a, -um** – lowest, i.e. bottom of; **pectus . . . sub imum** = *sub imum pectus*: 'under the bottom of her breast'.

109 **incumbo, -ere, incubui** – I fall on (+ dative); **ferrum, -i (n)** – sword; **quod** – which; **adhuc** – still; **caedes, -is (f)** – blood (i.e. Pyramus' blood); **tepeo, -ere** – I am warm.

110 **votum, -i (n)** – prayer; **tango, -ere, tetigi** – I touch (*tetigere* is the alternative perfect tense form of *tetigerunt*); **parens, -entis (m, f)** – parent.

111 **color, -oris (m)** – colour; **pomum, -i (n)** – fruit; **ubi** – when; **permaturio, -ire, -ui** – I ripen; **ater, atra, atrum** – dark red, black.

112 **quodque** = *et quod* – 'and whatever'; **rogus, -i (m)** – funeral pyre; **supersum, -esse** – I survive, remain; **quod . . . superest** – 'whatever remained of the funeral pyre', i.e. their ashes; **requiesco, -ere** – I rest; **urna, -ae (f)** – urn; **una . . . in urna** – a deliberate piece of word play on Ovid's part?

Figure 6 *A wall painting from Pompeii showing Pyramus and Thisbe under the mulberry tree, with Ninus' tomb in the background.*
Photo: Mondadori Portfolio/Contributor/Getty Images.

Pyramus and Thisbe in later literature

The most well-known version of Ovid's story appears in Shakespeare's comedy *A Midsummer Night's Dream* (Act 5, Scene 1). It is possible that Shakespeare had been reading the *Metamorphoses* when he wrote it, or at least a translation of it.

At the end of the play, some of the characters perform the story of Pyramus and Thisbe to entertain guests at a wedding, but the guests laugh at their bad performance as if they are watching a comedy. We might ask ourselves why Shakespeare chose to take this tragic tale of young love and put it into a comedy. Are there are any humorous elements in Ovid's own version?

The story of Pyramus and Thisbe may also be familiar from Shakespeare's tragedy *Romeo and Juliet*, in which two young lovers, prevented from meeting by their parents, also take their own life after a tragic misunderstanding.

Final questions

- In his story of Pyramus and Thisbe, how well does Ovid use direct speech and soliloquy?
- Some people see the main theme of the story as the loss of innocence. What do you think they mean by this?
- Is Ovid's description of the two lovers a sympathetic one?
- Does he show more interest in Thisbe than Pyramus?

Verse Literature B

2027–28 Prescription

This selection is taken from *Virgil*, Aeneid II, lines 1–56 and 195–253. The text is that of R. A. B. Mynors' edition in the Oxford Classical Text series, with minor changes of punctuation to help the GCSE student.

Virgil

Publius Vergilius Maro was born the son of a farmer in northern Italy in 70 BCE. He studied in Rome and Naples, and after a brief flirtation with law he became a writer. His first work, the *Eclogues*, was a collection of pastoral poems imitating the work of the Greek poet Theocritus. He soon gained a reputation as a poet and came to the attention of Maecenas, an influential literary patron with connections to Octavian, the future emperor Augustus.

From 37 BCE Virgil turned his attention to the *Georgics*, a long poem in four books outlining Roman methods of farming. All four books are dedicated to Maecenas and contain passages in praise of the future Augustus – they were written at a time when people were longing for the civil wars to end and peace to return after the turbulent latter period of the Roman Republic.

Around 30 BCE, Virgil began the *Aeneid*, a work intended to be a celebration of the Roman race, Roman virtues and the new era of peace and prosperity that Augustus would establish. Virgil took as his inspiration the *Iliad* and the *Odyssey*, epic tales composed by the Greek poet Homer, but the *Aeneid* is a thoroughly Roman work. It describes not only the suffering that Aeneas faced as a wandering refugee from Troy but also the glory of Roman history that was to follow his foundation of a new settlement in Italy. We see this most in Book VI, when Aeneas goes down to the Underworld and is shown the souls of great Romans yet to be born (but familiar to people of Virgil's own day). The *Aeneid* is therefore a truly national epic – it shows Virgil's contemporary audience that the Romans were not descended from some obscure Italian tribe but from a man who belonged to the golden age of heroes at the time of the Trojan War and who had the goddess Venus as his mother. It also deals with themes that have remained relevant to each successive generation of later readers: war, tragedy, love, loss, forced migration, determination in the face of suffering, duty to one's family and country, hope for a brighter future.

Virgil's method of composition was very different from Homer's. It is generally believed that Homer was a performing story-teller in a predominantly oral culture. Virgil, on the other hand, was very much the product of an educated, literary culture and he worked painstakingly slowly, so much so that when he died in 19 BCE the

Aeneid was still unfinished after more than ten years of work. The story goes that he gave orders on his deathbed for the *Aeneid* to be destroyed – luckily for us, it survived.

If you are a student coming to Virgil after only a short time of studying Latin, you may not find him easy, but we hope that you will enjoy the rewards of reading part of one of the greatest works of Western literature in the original Latin.

The story so far

Virgil begins the *Aeneid* with the famous words *arma virumque cano* ('I sing of arms and a man'). In twelve books he will tell how the Trojan prince Aeneas escaped from Troy when it was sacked by the Greeks after ten years of bitter war. Despite the opposition of the gods, especially the goddess Juno, but guided by his mother (the goddess Venus), Aeneas eventually reached Italy and fulfilled his mission to found a new Troy. 'This', wrote Virgil, 'was the beginning of the Latin race and the walls of lofty Rome.'

Book I opens in Carthage on the coast of North Africa. Carthage had been founded by Queen Dido, who, like Aeneas, was a refugee from further east. The goddess Juno, determined to keep the Trojans away from Italy, persuades Aeolus, king of the winds, to cause a storm which wrecks some of the Trojans' ships and drives Aeneas onto the coast.

Meanwhile, at the home of the gods on Mount Olympus, Venus asks Jupiter what the Trojans have done to deserve such suffering. Jupiter reassures her that Aeneas' destiny remains unchanged: he will reach Italy and found a city which will be the origin of Rome and the whole of the Roman Empire; one of his descendants will be none other than Julius Caesar. Jupiter sends the messenger god Mercury to make sure that Queen Dido will receive Aeneas hospitably.

With the help of his goddess mother, Aeneas finds his way from the shore to Dido's city. When he sees the decorations on the temple of Juno, which depict scenes from the Trojan War, he says to his friend Achates *sunt lacrimae rerum et mentem mortalia tangunt* ('there are tears in the nature of things and mortal suffering touches the heart', *Aeneid* I.462) – this may be taken as one of the main themes of the *Aeneid* as a whole. Aeneas' mission to found a new Troy in Italy involved suffering at every stage and Virgil involves us emotionally in his struggles to overcome it. This is particularly true of Book II, from which our selection is taken.

When Aeneas finally meets Dido, his effect on her is powerful: 'Dido was stunned, first at the sight of him, then at the great misfortune of the man' (*Aeneid* I.613–14). She leads him into her palace and preparations are made for a luxurious feast. At the feast, Dido invites him to tell his story: 'Come, guest, tell us from the beginning about the treachery of the Greeks, the sufferings of your people and your own wanderings' (*Aeneid* I.753ff.).

Aeneas' tale begins in Book II with how the Trojan War ended through the Greeks' trick of the wooden horse. The story of the war would have been familiar to Virgil's audience from the two great epics of the Greek poet Homer. His *Iliad* told how a Greek fleet had sailed to Troy to reclaim Helen, wife of King Menelaus, who had been abducted to Troy by the Trojan prince Paris. Ten years of war followed until the

Greek warrior Achilles killed Hector, son of the Trojan king Priam, and thus doomed Troy to its eventual sacking. The *Odyssey*, the second epic attributed to Homer, told of the return home of the Greek hero Odysseus (Ulysses to the Romans) after the war.

Our selection begins as Aeneas replies to Dido's request to tell his story.

Figure 7 *An artist's portrayal of the Trojan Horse being brought inside the gates of Troy.*
Photo: Getty Images.

Queen Dido has asked Aeneas to tell her about the fall of Troy; Aeneas now replies that his grief for Troy makes him reluctant to begin the tale. Besides, it is nearly morning.

conticuere omnes intentique ora tenebant;
inde toro pater Aeneas sic orsus ab alto:
'infandum, regina, iubes renovare dolorem,
Troianas ut opes et lamentabile regnum
eruerint Danai, quaeque ipse miserrima vidi　　　　　　　　　　5
et quorum pars magna fui. quis talia fando
Myrmidonum Dolopumve aut duri miles Ulixi
temperet a lacrimis? et iam nox umida caelo
praecipitat suadentque cadentia sidera somnos.
sed si tantus amor casus cognoscere nostros　　　　　　　　　　10
et breviter Troiae supremum audire laborem,
quamquam animus meminisse horret luctuque refugit,
incipiam.'

(*Aeneid* II.1–13)

Names and places

Aeneas, -ae (m): Aeneas – *pater* ('father') is a regular epithet (descriptive adjective) of Aeneas to show his responsibility as father not only to his son Ascanius but to the whole of his people.

Troianus, -a, -um: Trojan.

Danai, -aum (m pl): the Greeks (who were thought to be descended from Danaus).

Myrmidones, -um (m pl): the Myrmidons (Greek warriors led by Achilles).

Dolopes, -um (m pl): the Dolopians (Greek warriors led by Achilles' son Pyrrhus).

Ulixes, -i (m): Ulysses (the Latin name for the Greek hero Odysseus).

Troia, -ae (f): Troy.

Q. How does Aeneas show his pain about the fate of Troy and his reluctance to talk about it?

Q. Listen to the sound of line 9. How do the alliteration, assonance and the length of the words suggest the drowsiness of sleep?

GCSE vocabulary: *a/ab, altus, amor, animus, audio, brevis, cado, caelum, cognosco, et, fugio, iam, ipse, iubeo, labor, magnus, miles, miser, noster, nox, omnis, pars, pater, quamquam, qui/quae/quod, quis/quid, regina, regnum, sed, si, sic, talis, tantus, teneo, video.*

1   **conticesco, -ere, conticui** – I fall silent (*conticuere* is an alternative 3rd person plural perfect tense form for *conticuerunt* – the tense here may suggest the sudden silence as Aeneas begins to speak); **omnes** – 'everyone', i.e. the Trojans and Carthaginians attending Dido's feast; **intentus, -a, -um** – eager, attentive; **os, oris (n)** – face; **intentique ora tenebant** – literally 'and, attentive, held their faces': translate as 'and eagerly kept their gaze fixed on him'.

2   **inde** – then; **torus, -i (m)** – couch; **ordior, -iri, orsus sum** – I begin to speak (*orsus* = *orsus est*); **toro . . . ab alto** – 'from his lofty couch' (it is common for nouns to be split from their adjective like this in Latin poetry). Note that Dido has given Aeneas the honour of a special couch at the feast.

3   **infandus, -a, -um** – unspeakable; a strong word emphasized by its position at the start of the line; **regina** – i.e. Queen Dido; **iubes** – supply *me* as object; **renovo, -are** – I renew; **dolor, -oris (m)** – grief, pain; **infandum . . . dolorem** – notice how the noun is separated from its adjective. In this case the separation (known as hyperbaton*) has the effect of emphasizing both words.

4   **ut** – how (here introducing an indirect question *ut . . . eruerint*); **opes, -um (f pl)** – wealth, power; **lamentabilis, -e** – pitiable.

5   **eruo, -ere, -ui** – I overthrow (*eruerint* is perfect subjunctive in an indirect question: 'how the Greeks overthrew'); **quaeque . . . miserrima** – 'and the most pitiable things which'.

6   **et quorum . . . fui** – 'and of which I was a great part'(Aeneas' role in events is greater in the *Aeneid* than it was in Homer's *Iliad*); **quis** – 'which of' (take with the genitives *Myrmidonum Dolopumve*); **-ve** – or; **talia fando** – 'in telling such things'.

7   **aut** – or; **durus, -a, -um** – harsh; **miles** – with *miles* supply *quis*: 'which soldier . . .?'

8   **tempero, -are** – I refrain from (*temperet* is a potential subjunctive: 'could refrain'); **lacrima, -ae (f)** – tear; **umidus, -a, -um** – damp; **caelo** – 'from the sky' (the omission of a preposition like *ab/ex* is common in poetry).

9   **praecipito, -are** – I rush; **suadeo, -ere** – I urge; **sidus, -eris (n)** – star; **cadentia** – the stars are setting (literally 'falling'), i.e. it is nearly morning; **somnus, -i (m)** – sleep (take the plural as singular here, as often in poetry); **suadentque . . . somnos** – take time to analyse and hear the lovely sound of this line.

10 **tantus amor** – supply *tibi est* ('if you have such a great desire'); **cognoscere** – infinitive after *tantus amor tibi est*; **casus, -us (m)** – misfortune (*casus* is accusative plural).

11 **breviter** (adverb) – briefly; **audire** – also infinitive after *tantus amor tibi est*; **supremus, -a, -um** – last, final; **labor, -oris (m)** – take as 'pain' here.

12 **memini, -isse** – I remember *(meminisse* is a perfect infinitive with present meaning); **horreo, -ere** – I shudder (to do something); **luctus, -us (m)** – grief (take the ablative *luctu* as 'in grief'); **refugio, -ere, -fugi** – I flee from, recoil from *(refugit* is perfect tense here).

13 **incipio, -ere** – I begin (what tense is *incipiam*?).

Aeneas tells how the Greeks built a huge wooden horse, left it as an offering on the shore and sailed away to the nearby island of Tenedos.

        'fracti bello fatisque repulsi
ductores Danaum tot iam labentibus annis
instar montis equum divina Palladis arte   15
aedificant, sectaque intexunt abiete costas;
votum pro reditu simulant; ea fama vagatur.
huc delecta virum sortiti corpora furtim
includunt caeco lateri penitusque cavernas
ingentes uterumque armato milite complent.   20
est in conspectu Tenedos, notissima fama
insula, dives opum Priami dum regna manebant,
nunc tantum sinus et statio male fida carinis:
huc se provecti deserto in litore condunt;
nos abiisse rati et vento petiisse Mycenas.'   25

(*Aeneid* II.13–25)

Names and places

Danai, -aum (m pl): the Greeks.

Pallas, -adis (f): the goddess Pallas (Minerva), who was the goddess of wisdom and crafts and who sided with the Greeks in the war.

Tenedos, -i (f): Tenedos, an island a few miles from Troy.

Priamus, -i (m): Priam, king of Troy.

Mycenae, -arum (f pl): Mycenae, the home city of the Greek leader Agamemnon.

> Q. How does Virgil make Aeneas' tale fast-moving and interesting to hear?
> Q. Line 25: why do you think the Trojans were so quick to believe that the Greeks had really left for home?

GCSE vocabulary: *abeo, aedifico, annus, ars, bellum, corpus, dum, equus, et, iam, in, ingens, insula, is/ea/id, maneo, miles, mons, nos, nunc, peto, pro, -que, regnum, repello, se, sum, tantus, tot, vir.*

13 **frango, -ere, fregi, fractus** – I break (the perfect participles *fracti* and *repulsi* agree with *ductores*); **fatum, -i (n)** – fate. The neat order of *fracti bello fatisque repulsi* (participle–noun–noun–participle) is a good example of chiasmus*.

14 **ductor, -oris (m)** – leader; **tot** – take with *annis*; **labor, labi** – I fall, slip by (of time); **tot . . . labentibus annis** – 'as so many years slipped by'.

15 **instar montis** – 'the size of a mountain' (describing *equum*); **divinus, -a, -um** – divine (take *divina* as ablative with *arte*); **Palladis** – the horse had been built with the help of Minerva, sometimes known as Pallas.

16 **aedificant** – this is the first of a series of present tenses (writers often used the so-called 'historic' or 'vivid' present to describe past actions): it is fine to translate them as past tenses, as these notes do; **seco, secare, secui, sectus** – I cut (*secta* is ablative agreeing with *abiete*); **intexo, -ere** – I interweave; **abies, -etis (f)** – pine-wood; **costa, -ae (f)** – rib (the language comes from shipbuilding in which men 'weave' planks of wood to make the 'ribs' of a ship).

17 **votum, -i (m)** – offering; **reditus, -us (m)** – return; **simulo, -are** – I pretend (supply *eum esse*: 'they pretend that it is'); **fama, -ae (f)** – story; **vagor, -ari** – I go round; the *ea* is emphatic: '*this* is the story that goes round'.

18 **huc** – 'into this' (i.e. the horse); **delectus, -a, -um** – chosen (*delecta* agrees with *corpora*); **virum** = *virorum* (genitive); **sortior, -iri, sortitus sum** – I select; **furtim** – secretly (take with the verb *includunt* in the next line).

19 **includo, -ere** – I enclose (supply *eos* with *includunt*); **caecus, -a, -um** – dark, secret; **latus, -eris (n)** – side (the dative *lateri* is equivalent to *in* + accusative); **penitus** (adverb) – deep inside; **caverna, -ae (f)** – cavity (take *cavernas* with *ingentes* in the next line).

20 **uterus, -i (m)** – belly, womb (the horse is described in a metaphor* as being pregnant with soldiers); **armatus, -a, -um** – armed; **milite** – take as plural; **compleo, -ere** – I fill.

21 **conspectus, -us (m)** – sight (take *in conspectu* as 'within sight of Troy'); **Tenedos** – nominative; **notus, -a, -um** – well-known (*notissima* agrees with *insula*); **fama, -ae** – story (*fama* is ablative – 'most famous in storytelling').

22 **dives, -itis** – rich; **opes, -um (f pl)** – wealth, resources; **dives opum** – 'rich in resources'; **Priami** – genitive with *regna*; **dum** ('while') – conjunctions like this are often delayed in poetry (take it at the start of its clause); **regna** – plural for singular.

23 **tantum** (adverb) – only; **sinus, -us (m)** – bay; **statio, -onis (f)** – anchorage; **male fidus, -a, -um** – 'treacherous'; **carina, -ae (f)** – ship.

24 **huc** – to here; **provehor, -i, provectus sum** – I sail; **se** – take with *condunt*; **desertus, -a, -um** – deserted; **litus, -oris (n)** – shore; **condo, -ere** – I hide (*condunt* continues the sequence of vivid present tenses).

25 **nos** ('we') – subject of *rati (sumus)*; **reor, reri, ratus sum** – I think (take *rati* as *rati sumus* and supply *eos*: 'we thought that they . . .'); **abiisse . . . petiisse** – perfect infinitives of *abeo* and *peto* in an indirect statement after *rati*; **vento** – 'with a favourable wind'; **Mycenas** – the city of Mycenae stands for Greece as a whole here.

The Trojans opened their gates and went to inspect the remains of the Greek camp. When they saw the wooden horse, they were amazed at the sight, but there were conflicting opinions about what to do with it.

'ergo omnis longo solvit se Teucria luctu;
panduntur portae, iuvat ire et Dorica castra
desertosque videre locos litusque relictum:
hic Dolopum manus, hic saevus tendebat Achilles;
classibus hic locus, hic acie certare solebant.   30
pars stupet innuptae donum exitiale Minervae
et molem mirantur equi; primusque Thymoetes
duci intra muros hortatur et arce locari,
sive dolo seu iam Troiae sic fata ferebant.
at Capys, et quorum melior sententia menti,   35
aut pelago Danaum insidias suspectaque dona
praecipitare iubent subiectisque urere flammis,
aut terebrare cavas uteri et temptare latebras.
scinditur incertum studia in contraria vulgus.'

(*Aeneid* II.26–39)

Names and places

Teucria, -ae (f): the area of Troy (Teucer was an ancient king of Troy).

Doricus, -a, -um: Greek.

Dolopes, -um (m pl): the Dolopians (Greek warriors).

Achilles, -is (m): Achilles (the best fighter on the Greek side).

Minerva, -ae (f): the goddess Minerva.

Thymoetes, -ae (m): Thymoetes (a Trojan) – there was a legend that he had a grudge against Priam for killing his wife and son, so perhaps he had a motive for treachery.

Capys, -yos (m): Capys (a Trojan).

Danai, -aum (m pl): the Danaans, i.e. Greeks.

Q. *panduntur portae* (line 2) – a dramatic moment! How does Virgil make these words stand out?

Q. Notice the alliteration of *s* and *l* in line 1 – how does it add to the effect of the line? Notice also the prominence of long syllables – how do they reflect the meaning?

Q. How does Virgil draw attention to the Trojans' amazement at the horse and their conflicting views about what to do with it?

GCSE vocabulary: *castra, donum, duco, eo, equus, et, fero, hortor, iam, iubeo, locus, longus, manus, miror, omnis, pars, porta, primus, qui/quae/quod, relinquo, saevus, se, sic, soleo, video.*

26 **ergo** – therefore; **omnis ... Teucria** – 'the whole land of Troy' (i.e. not just the city); **solvo, solvere, solvi** – I set free, release (from); **luctus, -us (m)** – grief (*luctu* agrees with *longo* – take the ablative as *ex longo luctu*).

27 **pando, -ere** – I throw open; **iuvat** – it is pleasing to (supply *nos* and translate as 'we were pleased'); **ire ... videre** – infinitives dependent on *iuvat*; **Dorica castra ... desertos locos ... litus relictum** – all accusatives after *videre* (Virgil imagines the Trojans sightseeing round the remains of the Greek camp). Notice the order of the words to stress *desertos* and *relictum* – the Greeks are nowhere to be seen.

28 **desertus, -a, -um** – deserted; **litus, -oris (n)** – shore.

29 **hic** (adverb) – here; **manus, -us (f)** – band (of men); **tendo, -ere** – I make camp. What is the effect of *hic ... hic ... hic ... hic*?

30 **classis, -is (f)** – fleet (*classibus* is plural for singular); **locus** – supply *est* ('here was the place'); **acies, -ei (f)** – battle line (*acie* = *in acie*); **certo, -are** – I fight.

31 **pars, partis (f)** – part, i.e. 'some of them'; **stupeo, -ere** – I am amazed at; **innuptus, -a, -um** – unmarried (a traditional description of the virgin goddess Minerva); **Minervae** – dative (a gift 'for Minerva'); **exitialis, -e** – fatal (*exitiale* is neuter accusative singular agreeing with *donum*).

32 **moles, -is (f)** – huge size; note the switch to the 3rd plural in *mirantur*.

33 **duci ... locari** – present passive infinitives after *hortatur* (supply *eum* and translate 'urged it to be taken ... and placed'); **intra** (+ accusative) – inside; **arx, arcis (f)** – the citadel, i.e. the highest point of the city; **arce** = *in arce*; **loco, -are** – I place.

34 **sive ... seu** – whether ... or; **dolus, -i (m)** – deceit (translate the ablative *dolo* as 'through deceit'); **fatum, -i (n)** – fate (*fata* is nominative and subject of *ferebant*); **sic ... ferebant** – 'were going in that direction'.

35 **at** – but; **melior, -oris** – better (comparative of *bonus*); **sententia, -ae (f)** – opinion; **mens, mentis (f)** – mind; **et quorum ... menti** – supply *ei* and *est* and translate 'those *whose* mind had a better opinion'. After line 35 take *iubent* (line 37) as the main verb with *nos* understood as the object: 'Capys and those whose mind had a better opinion urged us ...'.

36 **aut ... aut** – either ... or; **pelagus, -i (n)** – sea (take the ablative *pelago* as 'into the sea'); **Danaum** is genitive plural (a contraction of *Danaorum*); **insidiae, -arum (f pl)** – treachery; **suspectus, -a, -um** – suspected; **dona** – neuter accusative plural.

37 **praecipito, -are** – I hurl; **subicio, subicere, subieci, subiectus** – I throw under; **uro, -ere** – I burn; **flamma, -ae (f)** – flame (*subiectis flammis* is instrumental ablative – 'to burn with flames put underneath them').

38 **terebro, -are** – I bore a hole through; **cavus, -a, -um** – hollow; **uterus, -i (m)** – womb, belly; **tempto, -are** – I test, try out; **latebra, -ae (f)** – hiding-place. The order of words is *aut terebrare et temptare cavas latebras uteri*. The idea was perhaps to prod spears into the holes of the horse to see if there was anyone inside.

39 **scindo, -ere** – I split; **incertus, -a, -um** – unsure (*incertum* agrees with the subject *vulgus*); **studia, -orum (n pl)** – factions, sides; **contrarius, -a, -um** – opposite (*contraria* agrees with *studia*); **vulgus, -i (n)** – the common people.

The priest Laocoon suddenly ran down from the citadel and warned the Trojans not to trust the Greeks or the horse.

'primus ibi ante omnes magna comitante caterva   40
Laocoon ardens summa decurrit ab arce,
et procul "o miseri, quae tanta insania, cives?
creditis avectos hostes? aut ulla putatis
dona carere dolis Danaum? sic notus Ulixes?
aut hoc inclusi ligno occultantur Achivi,   45
aut haec in nostros fabricata est machina muros,
inspectura domos venturaque desuper urbi,
aut aliquis latet error; equo ne credite, Teucri.
quidquid id est, timeo Danaos et dona ferentes."'

(*Aeneid* II.40–9)

Names and places

Laocoon, -ontis (m): Laocoon, a Trojan priest (pronounced as four syllables Lā-ŏc-ŏ-ōn).

Danai, -aum (m pl): the Danaans, i.e. Greeks.

Ulixes, -i (m): Ulysses (he was famous for his trickery and the wooden horse had been his idea).

Achivi, -orum (m pl): Achaeans (i.e. Greeks).

Teucri, -orum (m pl): Trojans (Teucer was an ancient king of Troy).

> Q.   How does Virgil show Laocoon's haste to warn the Trojans?
> Q.   What makes Laocoon's words so passionate?

GCSE vocabulary: *a/ab, civis, credo, domus, donum, duco, equus, et, fero, hic/haec/hoc, hostis, iam, ibi, in, is/ea/id, magnus, miser, murus, noster, omnis, primus, puto, quis/quid, sic, sum, summus, tantus, timeo, urbs, venio.*

40 **ante** (+ accusative) – before, in front of; **comitor, -ari** – I accompany; **caterva, -ae (f)** – crowd; **magna comitante caterva** is an ablative absolute ('with a great crowd accompanying him').

41 **ardeo, -ere** – I burn (note the metaphorical language to describe Laocoon's emotions); **decurro, -ere, -curri** – I run down from (note the urgency); **arx, arcis (f)** – citadel (the top of the city where the temples to Apollo and Minerva probably were).

42 **procul** – 'from a distance' (Laocoon's message is so urgent that he doesn't wait until he reaches the rest of the Trojans); understand a verb of saying with *et procul*; **o miseri** – Laocoon's dramatic speech begins with incredulous rhetorical questions* and ends with a memorable proverb; **o** – a common way of introducing an emotional exclamation; **miseri** – vocative with *cives*; **quae** – supply *est haec* ('what is this great madness?'); **tanta** = *magna* here; **insania, -ae (f)** – madness.

43 **avehor, -vehi, -vectus sum** – I sail away; **avectos** – supply *esse* and take as an indirect statement after *creditis* ('do you believe that . . .?'); **aut** – or; **ullus, -a, -um** – any (take *ulla* with *dona*).

44 **careo, -ere** (+ ablative) – I am without (take *carere* as infinitive in the indirect statement after *putatis* and translate 'do you think that any gifts are without . . .?'); **dolus, -i (m)** – trick; notice the emphatic alliteration* of *dona . . . dolis . . . Danaum*; **sic** – 'is this how'; **notus, -a, -um** – well-known (with *notus* supply *est vobis*). Note Laocoon's scornful tone. He does not know that the wooden horse was Ulysses' idea or that Ulysses was inside the horse at that very moment to hear his words, but he has made a good guess.

45 **aut . . . aut** – either . . . or; **includo, -ere, inclusi, inclusus** – I shut in; **lignum, -i (n)** – wood (notice that Laocoon treats the horse as just a 'piece of wood', rather than a sacred offering); **occulto, -are** – I hide. Laocoon's first suggestion that there are soldiers inside the horse is correct. Notice how the succession of long syllables adds weight to his point.

46 **haec** – take as nominative with *machina*; **in nostros . . . muros** – 'against our walls'; **fabrico, -are, -avi, -atus** – I build; **machina, -ae (f)** – a machine, contraption (it might suggest here a Roman siege engine used to besiege towns). The word order is *aut haec machina fabricata est in nostros muros*.

47 **inspicio, -ere, inspexi, inspectus** – I spy on (*inspectura* and *ventura* are good revision of future participles used to express purpose); **desuper** (adverb) – from above; **urbi** = *in urbem*. Notice the assonance* of *inspectura . . . ventura . . . urbi*.

48 **aliquis . . . error** – 'some other deception'; **lateo, -ere** – I lie hidden; **ne credite** = *nolite credere* ('do not trust'). Laocoon's speech could have ended with this warning but he adds a powerful line to conclude.

49 **quidquid** – whatever; **et** – good revision of the use of *et* to mean 'even' ('even when they are bearing gifts'); **dona** has the sense of 'religious offerings' as well as 'gifts' here. As Laocoon hammers his point home, notice the harsh consonance* of q/c, d and t: *equo ne credite, Teucri. quidquid id est, timeo Danaos et dona ferentes*.

The priest Laocoon hurled a spear into the side of the horse.

'sic fatus validis ingentem viribus hastam   50
in latus inque feri curvam compagibus alvum
contorsit. stetit illa tremens, uteroque recusso
insonuere cavae gemitumque dedere cavernae.
et, si fata deum, si mens non laeva fuisset,
impulerat ferro Argolicas foedare latebras,   55
Troiaque nunc staret, Priamique arx alta maneres.'

(*Aeneid* II.50–6)

Names and places
Argolicus, -a, -um: Greek.

Troia, -ae (f): Troy.

Priamus, -i (m): Priam, king of Troy.

> Q. How does the sound of the words in line 53 suggest the echoing sound the spear makes inside the horse?

GCSE vocabulary: *altus, deus, do, et, fui (sum), ille/illa/illud, in, ingens, maneo, mens, non, nunc, -que, si, sic, sto, validus.*

Sinon's deceit
In lines omitted from this selection (Aeneid II.57–194), Aeneas tells how some shepherds brought a prisoner to King Priam with his hands tied behind his back.

The prisoner claimed to be a Greek called Sinon who had angered Ulysses, one of the Greek leaders. According to Sinon, when an oracle had told the Greeks that they could only sail safely back to Greece if they sacrificed a life, they decided that he should be the victim. Sinon told Priam how he managed to escape just before being sacrificed; he had come to Troy as a deserter from the Greeks to ask for the Trojans' pity.

Priam ordered Sinon to be released and asked him what the wooden horse was for. Sinon told him that the Greeks had given up their attempt to take Troy and had set sail for home; to make up for violating the temple of the goddess Minerva, they had built the wooden horse as an offering to her.

Sinon's aim was for the Trojans to treat the horse as a religious offering and take it into the city, without knowing that it was full of Greek soldiers.

50 **fateor, fateri, fatus sum** – I speak; **vires, -ium (f pl)** – force (take *viribus* as ablative agreeing with *validis*); **hasta, -ae (f)** – spear (*hastam* is the direct object of *contorsit* in line 52).

51 **latus, -eris (n)** – side (of the horse); **ferus, -i (m)** – wild beast, monster (i.e. the horse); **curvus, -a, -um** – curved (*curvam* agrees with *alvum*); **compages, -is (f)** – fastening, joint (referring to the joints of pieces of wood fitted together); **alvus, -i (f)** – belly (one of a small number of 2nd declension *-us* nouns that are feminine not masculine); **curvam compagibus alvum** – 'the belly curved with joints'.

52 **contorqueo, -ere, contorsi** – I hurl; *contorsit* is as good an example of effective enjambment* as you will ever find: notice how lines 50–1, with their description of the mighty spear, the effort it took by Laocoon to wield it, and the wooden structure of the horse, all lead up to the climax of Laocoon hurling his spear violently into the side of the horse with the delayed verb *contorsit* – the three long syllables and strong word-break after it emphasize the verb further; **stetit** – 'it stood' i.e. 'stuck'; **illa (hasta)** – it, i.e. the spear; **tremo, -ere, -ui** – I tremble, shake (a vivid verb to describe the spear vibrating/quivering in the wood); **uterus, -i (m)** – womb (Virgil is fond of this word to describe the inside of the horse – see lines 20 and 38 – it uses the idea of pregnancy while suggesting that the 'birth' of the horse will bring death to the Trojans); **recutio, -ere, recussi, recussus** – I shake (*utero recusso* is an ablative absolute).

53 **insono, -are, -ui** – I resound, echo; **cavus, -a, -um** – hollow (take *cavae* with *cavernae* and pause to consider the echoing effect of the repetition *cavae . . . cavernae*); **gemitus, -us (m)** – groan (i.e. the echoing sound from inside the horse); **insonuere . . . dedere** – these are both alternative forms for the perfect tense *-erunt* and the assonance* of *-ere . . . -ere* adds to the sound effect of *cavae . . . cavernae*; **caverna, -ae (f)** – hole, cavity.

54 **fatum, -i (n)** – fate; **deum** = *deorum* (genitive plural); **mens, mentis (f)** – mind, intention (some scholars take this as referring to the 'feelings' of the Trojans but it is more likely to refer to the 'intention' of the gods); **laevus, -a, -um** – unfavourable (take with *mens*); **si . . . fuisset** is an example of a grammar construction not required for GCSE: a pluperfect subjunctive in a remote past conditional (if A had/had not happened, B would have/have not happened) – translate as 'if the fates of the gods and their intention had not been unfavourable'.

55 **impello, -ere, impuli** – I drive (normal grammar would require the subjunctive form *impulisset* ('he would have driven us'), but the indicative is used here to suggest that it was close to actually happening); **ferrum, -i (n)** – iron, i.e. sword; **foedo, -are** – I defile (as if the horse is a sacred object); **latebra, -ae (f)** – hiding-place.

56 **staret** – the tense of the conditional now changes to the imperfect to show what would be happening now ('and Troy would now still be standing'); **arx, arcis (f)** – citadel; **maneres** – the switch to the 2nd person as if the citadel of Priam is being addressed personally is unexpected and movingly dramatic ('and you, the lofty citadel of Priam, would still remain'). This is a striking example of apostrophe*.

Aeneas now tells Dido how the Trojans were taken in by Sinon's lies. Then something remarkable happened to the priest Laocoon.

'talibus insidiis periurique arte Sinonis
credita res, captique dolis lacrimisque coactis
quos neque Tydides nec Larisaeus Achilles,
non anni domuere decem, non mille carinae. 60
hic aliud maius miseris multoque tremendum
obicitur magis atque improvida pectora turbat.
Laocoon, ductus Neptuno sorte sacerdos,
sollemnes taurum ingentem mactabat ad aras.'

(*Aeneid* II.195–202)

Names and places
Sinon, -onis (m): Sinon (a Greek).

Tydides, -ae (m): son of Tydeus, i.e. Diomedes, a Greek warrior.

Larisaeus, -a, -um: Larissean (a description of Achilles who came from near the town of Larissa).

Achilles, -is (m): Achilles.

Laocoon, -ontis (m): Laocoon, the Trojan priest.

Neptunus, -i (m): Neptune (god of the sea and founder of Troy).

Sacrifice
In the ancient world, the killing of an animal and its dedication to a god were standard features of a religious ceremony designed to win the god's approval. In the description which follows there is a cruel twist as Laocoon and his sons themselves become sacrificial victims (see especially lines 85–6).

Why was Laocoon killed?
The Trojans clearly believed that Laocoon's death was Minerva's punishment for desecrating the horse with his spear. Were they right? To what extent does Virgil encourage us, his readers, to think that Laocoon was guilty?

> Q. In lines 57–60, how does Virgil stress the deceit of the Greeks and gullibility of the Trojans?

GCSE vocabulary: *ac/atque, ad, alius/alia/aliud, annus, ars, atque, capio, cogo, credo, decem, duco, ingens, mille, miser, multus, nec/neque, non, qui/quae/quod, res, talis.*

57 **insidiae, -arum (f pl)** – trick; **periurus, -a, -um** – lying, deceitful (take *periuri* as genitive with *Sinonis*); *insidiis* and *arte* are both instrumental ablatives ('through such tricks and the skill'). Notice the number of words in lines 57–8 relating to the theme of deceiving and being deceived, and the marked alliteration* of *c* (to show Aeneas' anger?).

58 **credita** – supply *est* (the subject of the verb is *res*); **res** – take here as 'the story' (notice how the enjambment* of *credita res* gives it emphasis); **capti** – supply *sumus*; **dolus, -i (m)** – deceit; **coactis** (from *cogo*) – 'forced', i.e. 'false'; **lacrima, -ae (f)** – tear.

59 **quos** is object of the verb *domuere*: 'we whom neither Tydides nor Larissean Achilles . . . subdued'.

60 **domo, -are, -ui** – I subdue (like *conticuere* in line 1, *domuere* is an alternative form for the 3rd person perfect *domuerunt*); **carina, -ae (f)** – ship; **mille carinae** – writers traditionally thought of the Greek fleet as having a thousand ships. The list of people and things which have so far failed to overcome the Trojans (*Tydides . . . Achilles . . . anni decem . . . mille carinae*) and the repetition of *neque . . . nec . . . non . . . non* draw attention to how easily the Trojans have been taken in by the lies of Sinon. Aeneas is clearly full of regret.

61 **hic** – 'at this point'; **aliud maius** – 'something greater'; **miseris** – supply *nobis* ('us in our misery'); **tremendus, -a, -um** – terrible; **multo** goes with **magis** in the next line ('much more terrible') – their separation perhaps serves to draw our attention to them; *maius miseris multoque tremendum* – the alliteration* of *m*, as often, suggests that something ominous is about to happen.

62 **obicio, -ere** – I throw onto (the subject is *aliud magis* in the previous line); **improvidus, -a, -um** – unforeseeing, unprepared; **pectus, -oris (n)** – chest, heart; **turbo, -are** – I disturb.

63 **ductus sorte** – 'drawn by lot'; **Neptuno** is dative; **sacerdos, -otis (m)** – priest; **ductus Neptuno sorte sacerdos** – 'drawn by lot as a priest to Neptune'.

64 **sollemnis, -e** – customary, established (take *sollemnes* as accusative plural agreeing with *aras*); **taurus, -i (m)** – bull; **macto, -are** – I sacrifice; **ad** – 'at'; **ara, -ae (f)** – altar (presumably set up on the shoreline).

Just as Laocoon was sacrificing at the altar of Neptune, two serpents were seen coming over the sea from the island of Tenedos.

'ecce autem gemini a Tenedo tranquilla per alta 65
(horresco referens) immensis orbibus angues
incumbunt pelago pariterque ad litora tendunt;
pectora quorum inter fluctus arrecta iubaeque
sanguineae superant undas, pars cetera pontum
pone legit sinuatque immensa volumine terga. 70
fit sonitus spumante salo; iamque arva tenebant
ardentesque oculos suffecti sanguine et igni
sibila lambebant linguis vibrantibus ora.'

(*Aeneid* II.203–11)

Names and places
Tenedos, -i (f): Tenedos.

> Q. What is the effect of *ecce* (line 65)?
> Q. How does Virgil suggest the huge size of the snakes?

GCSE vocabulary: *a/ab, ad, altus, ecce, et, iam, inter, lego, pars, per, -que, qui/quae/quod, sanguis, supero, teneo.*

Figure 8 *A marble statue of Laocoon and his sons (Vatican Museum, Rome).*
Photo: Print Collector/Contributor/Getty Images.

65 **autem** – but; **geminus, -a, -um** – twin, two (take with *angues* in the next line); **a Tenedo** – the snakes came from the island where the Greek ships had hidden; **tranquillus, -a, -um** – peaceful (i.e. the Trojans had no warning of what was about to happen); **alta** – take as an adjective used as a noun ('the depths').

66 **horresco, -ere** – I shudder (the 1st person form reminds us that it is Aeneas who is telling the tale); **refero, referre** (= *re* + *fero*) – I bring back, i.e. relate; **immensus, -a, -um** – huge; **orbis, orbis (m)** – coil; **anguis, -is (m/f)** – snake.

67 **incumbo, -ere** (+ dative) – I lean into (but take *incumbunt* here as 'made their way through' – note the vivid historic presents in 67–70); **pelagus, -i (n)** – sea; **pariter** – equally, i.e. side by side; **litus, -oris (n)** – shore; **tendo, -ere** – I make for.

68 **quorum pectora** – 'their chests' (*pectora* and *iubae* are the subjects of *superant*); **fluctus, -us (m)** – wave; **arrectus, -a, -um** – raised; **iuba, -ae (f)** – crest (e.g. of a helmet or serpent). Notice how the sound of the words in the next few lines adds to the dramatic effect: *pectore ... arrecta ... suffecti, superant ... spumante, tenebant ... lambebant ... vibrantibus, fit sonitus spumante salo*.

69 **sanguineus, -a, -um** – blood-red; **supero, -are** – I rise above; **unda, -ae (f)** – wave; **pars cetera** – 'the remaining part', i.e. 'the rest of them' (body and tail); **pontus, -i (m)** – sea. Notice the prominent alliteration* of *s* in lines 69–71 to suggest the hissing of the snakes.

70 **pone** – behind; **lego, -ere** – I pick my way through, go across; **sinuo, -are** – I bend, curve (the object is *terga*); **immensus, -a, -um** – huge; **volumen, -inis (n)** – coil (*volumine* is ablative = 'in a coil'); **tergum, -i (n)** – back.

71 **fio, fieri** – I happen; **sonitus, -us (m)** – sound; **fit sonitus** – 'there was a sound'; **spumo, -are** – I foam; **salum, -i (n)** – salt-sea; *spumante salo* is an ablative absolute – 'as the salt-sea foamed'; **arvum, -i (n)** – field, i.e. dry land; **tenebant** – 'they held', i.e. 'they had reached'.

72 **ardeo, -ere** – I blaze; **oculus, -i (m)** – eye; **suffectus, -a, -um** – I suffuse, tinge; *ardentes oculos* is an accusative of respect depending on *suffecti* – 'tinged in their blazing eyes', i.e. 'with their blazing eyes tinged with ...'; **ignis, -is (m)** – fire.

73 **sibilus, -a, -um** – hissing (*sibila* agrees with *ora*); **lambo, -ere** – I lick; **lingua, -ae (f)** – tongue; **vibro, -are** – I flicker; **os, oris (n)** – mouth.

The serpents brutally attacked Laocoon and his sons before taking refuge in the citadel of Minerva.

'diffugimus visu exsangues. illi agmine certo
Laocoonta petunt; et primum parva duorum 75
corpora natorum serpens amplexus uterque
implicat et miseros morsu depascitur artus;
post ipsum auxilio subeuntem ac tela ferentem
corripiunt spirisque ligant ingentibus; et iam
bis medium amplexi, bis collo squamea circum 80
terga dati superant capite et cervicibus altis.
ille simul manibus tendit divellere nodos
perfusus sanie vittas atroque veneno,
clamores simul horrendos ad sidera tollit:
qualis mugitus, fugit cum saucius aram 85
taurus et incertam excussit cervice securim.
at gemini lapsu delubra ad summa dracones
effugiunt saevaeque petunt Tritonidis arcem,
sub pedibusque deae clipeique sub orbe teguntur.'

(*Aeneid* II.212–27)

Names and places
Laocoon, -ontis (acc. **Laocoonta**) (**m**): Laocoon.

Tritonis, -idis (**f**): Minerva (she was supposedly born near Lake Tritonis).

Q. *diffugimus ... petunt* (lines 74–5): what is the effect of these two short sentences?

Q. How well does Virgil describe the snakes' attack in lines 75–84?

Q. What is suggested by the fact that the snakes escape to the temple of Minerva?

Q. Why do you think that Virgil chose not to describe Laocoon's actual death?

GCSE vocabulary: *a/ab, ac/atque, ad, altus, auxilium, caput, circum, clamor, corpus, cum, dea, do, duo, ecce, effugio, et, fero, fugio, iam, ille, ingens, inter, ipse, manus, medius, miser, pars, parvus, per, pes, peto, qualis, -que, qui/quae/quod, saevus, simul, sub, summus, supero, teneo, tollo.*

74 **diffugio, -ere** – I flee in different directions; **visus, -us (m)** – sight (*visu* = 'at the sight'); **exsanguis, -e** – pale; **illi** – i.e. the snakes; **agmen, -inis (n)** – line; **certus, -a, -um** – straight; **agmine certo** – 'in a straight line' (does this military term suggest the impending advance of the Greek soldiers?).

76 **natus, -i (m)** – son; **serpens, -entis (m/f)** – snake; **amplexus, -a, -um** – encircling; **uterque, utraque, utrumque** – each (take with *serpens*).

77 **implico, -are** – I entwine myself around (take *parva corpora* as the object); **morsus, -us (m)** – biting; **depascor, -i** – I feed on; **morsu depascitur** – 'fed on by biting' i.e. 'devoured'; **artus, -us (m)** – limb.

78 **post** – an adverb here: 'afterwards'; **ipsum** – 'Laocoon himself' (object of *corripiunt*); **auxilio subeo, -ire, -ii** – I come to help; **telum, -i (n)** – weapon.

79 **corripio, -ere** – I seize (notice the enjambment*); **spira, -ae (f)** – coil; **ligo, -are** – I tie up, surround.

80 **bis** – twice; **medium** – 'his middle'; **amplector, -i, amplexus sum** – I wind myself round; **collum, -i (n)** – neck; **squameus, -a, -um** – scaly.

81 **tergum, -i (n)** – back, i.e. body; **circum ... do** – I put around; **collo squamea circum terga dati** –'having put their scaly bodies around his neck' (the perfect passive participle *circumdati* has an active sense here); **supero, -are** – I rise above; **cervix, -icis (f)** – neck; **capite et cervicibus altis** – 'with their heads and tall necks' (referring to the snakes).

82 **ille** – i.e. Laocoon (a sudden change of subject); **tendo, -ere** – I try; **divello, -ere** – I tear apart; **nodus, -i (m)** – knot.

83 **perfundo, -ere, perfudi, perfusus** – I drench; **sanies, -ei (f)** – gore (a vivid choice to describe Laocoon's own blood); **vitta, -ae (f)** – headband (worn as a holy object by a priest and expected to be kept clean); **perfusus sanie vittas** – 'with his headbands drenched in gore' (lit. 'drenched in gore with respect to his headbands'); **ater, atra, atrum** – dark; **venenum, -i (n)** – poison.

84 **horrendus, -a, -um** – terrible; **sidus, -eris (n)** – star.

85 **mugitus, -us (m)** – bellowing; **qualis mugitus (est)** – 'it was like the bellowing'; **cum** – when (take it immediately after *qualis mugitus*); **fugit** – perfect tense, like *excussit* in the next line ('has fled ... has shaken off'); **saucius, -a, -um** – wounded (it agrees with *taurus* in the next line); **ara, -ae (f)** – altar (the bull is clearly about to be sacrificed in a religious ritual). Notice the bellowing *u* sounds of *mugitus ... fugit*.

86 **taurus, -i (m)** – bull; **incertus, -a, -um** – uncertain, badly aimed; **excutio, -ere, -cussi** – I shake off; **cervix, -icis (f)** – neck (*cervice* is ablative: 'from its neck'); **securis, -is (f)** – axe (*securim* is accusative and object of *excussit*).

87 **at** – but; **geminus, -a, -um** – two (take with *dracones*); **lapsus, -us (m)** – slithering (take with *effugiunt* in the next line and translate as 'slithered away'); **delubrum, -i (n)** – temple, shrine; **draco, -onis (m)** – snake.

88 **arx, arcis (f)** – citadel.

89 **clipeus, -i (m)** – shield; **orbs, orbis (m)** – circle (of a shield); **tego, -ere** – I cover, hide (the passive *teguntur* has the sense of 'hide themselves'). Notice the rapid movement of this line created by the maximum number of dactyls (see pp. xiv–xv).

The Trojans, who now thought that Laocoon had been punished for violating the horse with his spear, decided to bring the horse up to the walls of the city.

'tum vero tremefacta novus per pectora cunctis   90
insinuat pavor, et scelus expendisse merentem
Laocoonta ferunt, sacrum qui cuspide robur
laeserit et tergo sceleratam intorserit hastam.
ducendum ad sedes simulacrum orandaque divae
numina conclamant.   95
dividimus muros et moenia pandimus urbis.
accingunt omnes operi pedibusque rotarum
subiciunt lapsus, et stuppea vincula collo
intendunt; scandit fatalis machina muros
feta armis. pueri circum innuptaeque puellae   100
sacra canunt funemque manu contingere gaudent;
illa subit mediaeque minans inlabitur urbi.'

(*Aeneid* II.228–40)

Names and places
Laocoon, -ontis (acc. -onta) (m): Laocoon.

Half lines
Line 95 is one of a number of lines in the *Aeneid* that are incomplete – they show that Virgil's work was unfinished at the time of his death.

Festivals
Typical features of a religious procession were young people pulling carts with images of the gods and singing sacred songs in a general atmosphere of joy and celebration. It is therefore grimly ironic that the 'image' they bring into Troy is a war machine (*machina*) full of armed men (*feta armis*).

Q. How does Virgil emphasize the fear of the Trojans and their view that Laocoon had been deservedly punished (lines 90–3)?

Q. Why do you think Aeneas suddenly switches to the 1st person in *dividimus* and *pandimus* in line 96?

Q. In lines 96–102 how does Virgil suggest a sense of rapid activity and joyous celebration?

GCSE vocabulary: *arma, clamo, duco, et, fero, gaudeo, ille/illa/illud, manus, medius, murus, novus, omnis, oro, per, pes, puella, puer, -que, qui/quae/quod, sacer, scelus, tum, urbs.*

90   vero – indeed; **tremefactus, -a, -um** – terrified (take with *pectora*); **novus** ('new') agrees with *pavor* in the next line; **pectus, -oris (n)** – heart; **cunctus, -a, -um** – all (take the dative *cunctis* = 'of everyone').

91   **insinuo, -are** – I penetrate; **pavor, -oris (m)** – fear; **scelus, -eris (n)** – crime; **expendo, -ere, expendi** – I pay for; **mereo, -ere** – I deserve (the participle *merentem* agrees with the accusative *Laocoonta* but might be translated as an adverb here: 'deservedly').

92   **ferunt** – beyond the usual meanings of 'bring/carry/bear', *fero* can mean 'I relate, say' (it introduces an indirect statement here: 'they said that Laocoon ...'); **sacrum ... laeserit** – the order is *qui laeserit sacrum robur;* **qui** – the perfect subjunctives *laeserit* and *intorserit* suggest the reason for Laocoon's punishment: translate *qui* as 'because he ...'; **sacrum** – the horse is now a sacred object in the eyes of the Trojans; **cuspis, -idis (f)** – spear; **robur, -oris (n)** – oak, i.e. the wooden horse.

93   **laedo, -ere, laesi** – I harm; **tergum, -i (n)** – back (*tergo* = 'at its back'); **sceleratus, -a, -um** – wicked, unholy (a strong word); **intorqueo, -ere, intorsi** – I hurl; **hasta, -ae (f)** – spear.

94   The order is *conclamant simulacrum ducendum (esse) ad sedes (et) numina divae oranda (esse);* the gerundives *ducendum* and *oranda* are part of an indirect statement after *conclamant* ('they shouted that the image must be taken ...'); **sedes, -is (f)** – temple; **simulacrum, -i (n)** – image (i.e. the horse); **oro, -are** – I beg, pray for; **diva, -ae (f)** – goddess.

95   **numen, -inis (n)** – goodwill, favour (take the plural *numina* as singular); **conclamo, -are** – I shout.

96   A short, factual sentence marks the moment when Troy's fate is sealed; *dividimus* begins a series of eight vivid/historic presents showing the rapid activity of the Trojans; **divido, -ere** – I make a hole through (notice the sudden switch to the 1st person); **moenia, -ium (n pl)** – fortifications; **pando, -ere** – I open up.

97   **accingo, -ere** (+ dative) – I equip myself for; **opus, -eris (n)** – task; **rota, -ae (f)** – wheel.

98   **subicio, -ere** – I put under (take with *pedibus*, which refers to the feet of the horse); **lapsus, -us (m)** – gliding; **rotarum ... lapsus** – 'the glidings of the wheels', i.e. 'gliding wheels'; **stuppeus, -a, -um** – made of tow (a fibre used to make ropes); **vinculum, -i (n)** – chain, rope; **collum, -i (n)** – neck (*collo* is ablative: 'around its neck').

99   **intendo, -ere** – I stretch tight; **scando, -ere** – I climb; **fatalis, -e** – fateful; **machina, -ae (f)** – contraption (here suggesting an engine of war). Note the slow-moving rhythm of this line (five spondees) as the horse is slowly wheeled up through the walls into the city.

100 **fetus, -a, -um** – pregnant with (for the metaphor* see *uterum* in line 20); **circum** (adverb) – all around; **innuptus, -a, -um** – unmarried.

101 **sacra, -orum (n pl)** – sacred songs; **cano, -ere** – I sing; **funis, -is (m)** – rope; **contingo, -ere** – I touch.

102 **illa** (*machina*) – the horse; **subeo, -ire** – I go up; **minor, -ari** – I tower over, threaten (the present participle *minans* could be translated as an adverb 'threateningly'); **inlabor, -labi** (+ dative) – I slide into (take *mediae urbi* as the object).

Aeneas laments the fate of Troy as he tells how the Trojans brought the horse inside the gates. Even the prophetess Cassandra was unable to warn them.

'o patria, o divum domus Ilium et incluta bello
moenia Dardanidum! quater ipso in limine portae
substitit atque utero sonitum quater arma dedere;   105
instamus tamen immemores caecique furore
et monstrum infelix sacrata sistimus arce.
tunc etiam fatis aperit Cassandra futuris
ora dei iussu non umquam credita Teucris.
nos delubra deum miseri, quibus ultimus esset   110
ille dies, festa velamus fronde per urbem.
vertitur interea caelum et ruit Oceano nox
involvens umbra magna terramque polumque
Myrmidonumque dolos; fusi per moenia Teucri
conticuere; sopor fessos complectitur artus.'   115

(*Aeneid* II.241–53)

Names and places

Ilium, -i (n): Ilium, another name for Troy.

Dardanidae, -arum/-um (m pl): the Trojans (who were descended from Dardanus).

Cassandra, -ae (f): Cassandra, daughter of King Priam and Queen Hecuba, who had been punished by Apollo so that she would always prophesy the truth but never be believed.

Teucri, -orum (m pl): the Trojans.

Oceanus, -i (m): the Ocean.

Myrmidones, -um (m pl): the Greeks.

Q. What is the effect of the repeated *o* in line 103?
Q. In lines 106–7, how does Aeneas suggest the foolishness of the Trojans?
Q. How does the rhythm of line 107 add to the meaning?
Q. Why do you think Aeneas mentions Cassandra?

GCSE vocabulary: *ac/atque, arma, bellum, caelum, credo, deus, dies, do, domus, et, etiam, futurus (sum), ille, infelix, interea, ipse, magnus, miser, non, nos, nox, patria, per, porta, qui/quae/quod, sum, tamen, terra, umquam, urbs, verto.*

103 **o** introduces an emotive exclamation (see also line 42); **divus, -i (m)** – god (*divum* is genitive plural); **inclutus, -a, -um** – famous; **bello** – 'in war'. For all its devotion to the gods, Troy is still falling. Aeneas' high emotions are clear: notice the tricolon* of *o patria, o divum domus Ilium et incluta bello moenia Dardanidum*, with its alliteration* of *d* and assonance* of *-um*.

104 **moenia, -ium (n pl)** – walls, fortifications; **quater** (adverb) – four times; **limen, -inis (n)** – threshold.

105 **subsisto, -ere, substiti** – I halt (stumbling on a doorstep was a Roman symbol of bad luck); **uterus, -i (m)** – womb, belly (supply *ex* with *utero*); **sonitus, -i (m)** – sound; **dedere** = *dederunt* (the subject is *arma*).

106 **insto, -are** – I press on, hurry forward (notice the sudden switch to the vivid present after the perfect *dedere*); **immemor, -oris** – thoughtless; **caecus, -a, -um** – blind; **furor, -oris (m)** – frenzy, madness.

107 **monstrum, -i (n)** – monster (to Aeneas it is no longer a sacred object); **infelix, -icis** – unfortunate; **sacratus, -a, -um** – holy (take *sacrata* with *arce* and ask yourself whether Virgil deliberately puts *infelix* and *sacrata* next to each other); **sisto, -ere** – I set up, place; **arx, arcis (f)** – citadel (*arce* = *in arce*).

108 **tunc etiam** – 'then also'; **fatum, -i (n)** – fate; **aperio, -ire** – I open (*ora* is the object); **futurus, -a, -um** – future participle of *sum*: take *futuris* with *fatis* and translate as 'Cassandra opened her mouth for the fates which were to come', i.e. she began to foretell the future.

109 **os, oris (n)** – mouth (*ora* is plural for singular); **iussus, -us (m)** – order; **dei iussu** – 'by the order of the god' (i.e. Apollo); **credita** (perfect passive participle of *credo*) – take as agreeing with *ora*; **non umquam credita Teucris** – 'never believed by the Trojans'.

110 **delubrum, -i (n)** – shrine (*delubra* is object of *velamus*); **deum** = *deorum*; **nos ... quibus** – we ... for whom; **ultimus, -a, -um** – last; **esset** – imperfect subjunctive of *sum* ('it would be').

111 **festus, -a, -um** – festive (*festa* agrees with *fronde*); **velo, -are** – I cover; **frons, frondis (f)** – foliage, leaves; **per** (+ accusative) – (here) throughout.

112 **vertitur caelum** – the start of night was believed to be due to the sky turning rather than the earth; **ruo, -ere** – I rush; **Oceano** = *ex Oceano*.

113 **involvo, -ere** – I enclose (the participle *involvens* agrees with *nox* and has *terram, polum* and *dolos* as its objects); **umbra, -ae (f)** – darkness (*umbra* is ablative and has *magna* agreeing with it); **-que ... -que** – both ... and; **polus, -i (m)** – sky. Notice the ominous succession of long syllables in *involvens umbra magna* and alliteration* of *m* in lines 113–14.

114 **Myrmidonum** – genitive, dependent on *dolos*; **dolus, -i (m)** – treachery (*dolos* is plural for singular); **fusus, -a, -um** – scattered (*fusi* agrees with *Teucri*); **moenia, -ium (n pl)** – (here) buildings.

115 **conticesco, -ere, conticui** – I fall silent; **conticuere** = *conticuerunt*: the perfect tense and run-on position perhaps suggests the Trojans' sudden collapse into sleep (see line 1); **sopor, -oris (m)** – sleep; **fessus, -a, -um** – tired; **complector, -i** – I surround; **artus, -us (m)** – limb. Our selection thus ends with an ominous calm before the storm – even as the exhausted Trojans collapse into sleep (foreshadowing their imminent deaths?) the Greek ships are on their way back to Troy and their soldiers are about to pour out of the wooden horse. Troy is doomed.

What happens next?

In the rest of Book II, Aeneas describes to Dido the entry of the Greek soldiers into Troy. He tells how King Priam was brutally killed while sheltering with his wife at an altar and how the city was set on fire. Aeneas escaped with his old father Anchises, his young son Ascanius (also known as Iulus) and the household gods. Aeneas' wife Creusa was tragically lost on the way out of the city, but her ghost appeared to him and reassured him that his destiny was secure – he was destined to found a new kingdom in Italy.

In Book III Aeneas concludes his narrative to Queen Dido with the tale of his wanderings from Troy until reaching the shore of Africa and the city of Carthage.

Book IV tells the tragic tale of love-sick Queen Dido. When Aeneas is in danger of staying with her in Carthage and abandoning his mission, Jupiter prompts him to leave and continue his journey to Italy. He tries to do so secretly, but Dido finds out and attempts to persuade him to stay. Aeneas remains unmoved and, as his ships sail away, Dido takes her own life.

After sailing to Sicily, where Aeneas' father Anchises dies (Book V), Aeneas reaches Italy and travels down to the Underworld (Book VI), just as Odysseus had done in Homer's *Odyssey*. There he meets the ghost of his father Anchises, who shows him the souls of many of the great figures of Roman history down to Virgil's own time who are yet to be born.

Books VII to XII tell of Aeneas' welcome in Italy by the local king Latinus, who sees him as the future husband for his daughter Lavinia. Turnus, to whom Lavinia had been promised, is enraged and war begins between the Trojan and the Latins.

The *Aeneid* ends with a single combat duel between Aeneas and Turnus, just as Homer's *Iliad* had culminated in the duel between Achilles and Hector. In an uncharacteristic fit of anger, Aeneas kills Turnus. The last line of the poem tells how Turnus' life 'left him with a groan and fled indignantly down to the shades' (*vitaque cum gemitu fugit indignata sub umbras*, *Aeneid* XII.952).

Final questions

- How effective is it that Virgil puts his narrative about the Trojan Horse into the mouth of Aeneas in Dido's palace?
- Does Virgil present the Trojans as responsible for their own downfall?
- What are Virgil's strengths as a story-teller?

OCR LATIN GCSE DEFINED VOCABULARY LIST

a, ab + *ablative* (*also used as prefix with verbs*) — from, away from, by (as prefix = away)
absum, abesse, afui — be absent, be away, be distant from
ac, atque (*indeclinable*) — and
accido, accidere, accidi — happen
accipio, accipere, accepi, acceptus — accept, take in, receive
ad + *accusative* (*also used as prefix with verbs*) — to, towards, at
adeo (*indeclinable*) — so much, so greatly, to such an extent
adsum, adesse, adfui — be here, be present
advenio, advenire, adveni — arrive
aedifico, aedificare, aedificavi, aedificatus — build
ager, agri, m — field
ago, agere, egi, actus — do, act, drive
alii . . . alii — some . . . others
alius, alia, aliud — other, another, else
alter, altera, alterum — the other, another, one (of two), the second (of two)
altus, alta, altum — high, deep
ambulo, ambulare, ambulavi — walk
amicus, amici, m — friend
amo, amare, amavi, amatus — love, like
amor, amoris, m — love
ancilla, ancillae, f — slave-girl, slave-woman
animus, animi, m — spirit, soul, mind
annus, anni, m — year
antea (*indeclinable*) — before
appropinquo, appropinquare, appropinquavi + *dative* — approach, come near to
aqua, aquae, f — water
arma, armorum, n pl. — arms, weapons
ars, artis, f — art, skill

Latin	English
ascendo, ascendere, ascendi, ascensus	climb
audax, audacis	bold, daring
audeo, audere, ausus sum	dare
audio, audire, audivi, auditus	hear, listen to
aufero, auferre, abstuli, ablatus	take away, carry off, steal
auxilium, auxilii, n	help
bellum, belli, n	war
bene (*indeclinable*)	well
bibo, bibere, bibi	drink
bonus, bona, bonum	good
brevis, breve	short, brief
cado, cadere, cecidi, casus	fall
caelum, caeli, n	sky, heaven
capio, capere, cepi, captus	take, catch, capture, make (a plan)
captivus, captivi, m	captive, prisoner
caput, capitis, n	head
castra, castrorum, n pl.	camp
celer, celeris, celere	quick, fast
celo, celare, celavi, celatus	hide
cena, cenae, f	dinner, meal
ceteri, ceterae, cetera	the rest, the others
cibus, cibi, m	food
circum + *accusative*	around
civis, civis, m and f	citizen
clamo, clamare, clamavi, clamatus	shout
clamor, clamoris, m	shout, shouting, noise
clarus, clara, clarum	famous, clear
coepi, coepisse	began
cogito, cogitare, cogitavi, cogitatus	think, consider
cognosco, cognoscere, cognovi, cognitus	get to know, find out
cogo, cogere, coegi, coactus	force, compel
comes, comitis, m and f	comrade, companion
conficio, conficere, confeci, confectus	finish, wear out
conor, conari, conatus sum	try
consilium, consilii, n	plan, idea, advice
conspicio, conspicere, conspexi, conspectus	catch sight of, notice
constituo, constituere, constitui, constitutus	decide
consul, consulis, m	consul
consumo, consumere, consumpsi, consumptus	eat

contra + *accusative*	against
convenio, convenire, conveni	come together, gather, meet
copiae, copiarum, f pl.	forces, troops
corpus, corporis, n	body
cras (*indeclinable*)	tomorrow
credo, credere, credidi, creditus + *dative*	believe, trust
crudelis, crudele	cruel
cum + *ablative*	with
cum (*indeclinable*)	when, since
cupio, cupere, cupivi, cupitus	want, desire
cur? (*indeclinable*)	why?
cura, curae, f	care, worry
curro, currere, cucurri, cursus	run
custodio, custodire, custodivi, custoditus	guard
custos, custodis, m and f	guard
de + *ablative*	from, down from, about
dea, deae, f	goddess
debeo, debere, debui, debitus	owe, ought, should, must
defendo, defendere, defendi, defensus	defend
deinde (*indeclinable*)	then
deleo, delere, delevi, deletus	destroy
descendo, descendere, descendi, descensus	go down, come down
deus, dei, m	god
dico, dicere, dixi, dictus	say, speak, tell
dies, diei, m	day
difficilis, difficile	difficult
diligens, diligentis	careful
dirus, dira, dirum	dreadful
discedo, discedere, discessi	depart, leave
diu (*indeclinable*)	for a long time
do, dare, dedi, datus	give
doceo, docere, docui, doctus	teach
domina, dominae, f	mistress
dominus, domini, m	master
domus, domus f	home (domi = at home)
donum, doni, n	gift, present
dormio, dormire, dormivi	sleep
duco, ducere, duxi, ductus	lead, take
dum (*indeclinable*)	while, until
dux, ducis, m	leader

e, ex + *ablative* (*also used as prefix with verbs*)	from, out of, out
ecce! (*indeclinable*)	look!
effugio, effugere, effugi	escape
ego, mei	I, me
egredior, egredi, egressus sum	go out
emo, emere, emi, emptus	buy
enim (*indeclinable*)	for
eo, ire, i(v)i	go
epistula, epistulae, f	letter
equus, equi, m	horse
et (*indeclinable*)	and, even
et . . . et (*indeclinable*)	both . . . and
etiam (*indeclinable*)	also, even
exercitus, exercitus, m	army
exspecto, exspectare, exspectavi, exspectatus	wait for, expect
facilis, facile	easy
facio, facere, feci, factus	make, do
faveo, favere, favi, fautus + *dative*	favour, support
felix, felicis, fortunate	happy
femina, feminae, f	woman
fero, ferre, tuli, latus	bring, carry, bear
ferox, ferocis	fierce, ferocious
festino, festinare, festinavi	hurry
fidelis, fidele	faithful, loyal
filia, filiae, f	daughter
filius, filii, m	son
flumen, fluminis, n	river
forte (*indeclinable*)	by chance
fortis, forte	brave
forum, fori, n	forum, market place
frater, fratris, m	brother
frustra (*indeclinable*)	in vain
fugio, fugere, fugi	run away, flee
gaudeo, gaudere, gavisus sum	be pleased, rejoice
gaudium, gaudii, n	joy, pleasure
gens, gentis, f	family, tribe, race, people
gero, gerere, gessi, gestus	wear (clothes), wage (war)
gladius, gladii, m	sword
gravis, grave	heavy, serious

habeo, habere, habui, habitus	have, hold
habito, habitare, habitavi, habitatus	live
heri (*indeclinable*)	yesterday
hic, haec, hoc	this, he, she, it
hodie (*indeclinable*)	today
homo, hominis, m	man, human being
hora, horae, f	hour
hortor, hortari, hortatus sum	encourage, urge
hortus, horti, m	garden
hostis, hostis, m	enemy
iaceo, iacere, iacui	lie
iacio, iacere, ieci, iactus (*in compounds -icio*)	throw
iam (*indeclinable*)	now, already
ianua, ianuae, f	door
ibi (*indeclinable*)	there
idem, eadem, idem	the same
igitur (*indeclinable*)	therefore, and so
ille, illa, illud	that, he, she, it
imperator, imperatoris, m	emperor, general, leader
imperium, imperii, n	empire, power, command
impero, imperare, imperavi, imperatus + *dative*	order, command
in + *ablative (also used as prefix with verbs)*	in, on
in + *accusative (also used as prefix with verbs)*	into, onto
incendo, incendere, incendi, incensus	burn, set on fire
infelix, infelicis	unlucky, unhappy
ingens, ingentis	huge
ingredior, ingredi, ingressus sum	enter
inimicus, inimici, m	enemy
inquit	he/she says, he/she said
insula, insulae, f	island, block of flats
intellego, intellegere, intellexi, intellectus	understand, realize
inter + *accusative*	among, between
interea (*indeclinable*)	meanwhile
interficio, interficere, interfeci, interfectus	kill
intro, intrare, intravi, intratus	enter
invenio, invenire, inveni, inventus	find
invito, invitare, invitavi, invitatus	invite
ipse, ipsa, ipsum	himself, herself, itself, themselves

ira, irae, f	anger
iratus, irata, iratum	angry
is, ea, id	this, that, he, she, it, them
ita (*indeclinable*)	in this way, to such an extent, so
itaque (*indeclinable*)	and so, therefore
iter, itineris, n	journey
iterum (*indeclinable*)	again
iubeo, iubere, iussi, iussus	order
iuvenis, iuvenis, m	young man
labor, laboris, m	work, toil
laboro, laborare, laboravi	work, toil
lacrimo, lacrimare, lacrimavi	weep, cry
laetus, laeta, laetum	happy
laudo, laudare, laudavi, laudatus	praise
legio, legionis, f	legion
lego, legere, legi, lectus	read, choose
lentus, lenta, lentum	slow
libenter (*indeclinable*)	willingly, gladly
liber, libri, m	book
liberi, liberorum, m pl.	children
libero, liberare, liberavi, liberatus	set free
libertus, liberti, m	freedman, ex-slave
locus, loci, m	place
longus, longa, longum	long
loquor, loqui, locutus sum	speak, talk
lux, lucis, f	light, daylight
magnus, magna, magnum	big, large, great
malo, malle, malui	prefer
malus, mala, malum	evil, bad
maneo, manere, mansi	remain, stay
manus, manus, f	hand, group of people
mare, maris, n	sea
maritus, mariti, m	husband
mater, matris, f	mother
maxime (*indeclinable*)	very greatly
medius	media, medium, middle
meus, mea, meum	my
miles, militis, m	soldier
minime (*indeclinable*)	very little, least, no
miror, mirari, miratus sum	wonder at, admire

miser, misera, miserum	miserable, wretched, sad
mitto, mittere, misi, missus	send
modus, modi, m	manner, way, kind
moneo, monere, monui, monitus	warn, advise
mons, montis, m	mountain
morior, mori, mortuus sum	die
mors, mortis, f	death
moveo, movere, movi, motus	move
mox (*indeclinable*)	soon
multo (*indeclinable*)	much
multus, multa, multum	much, many
murus, muri, m	wall
nam (*indeclinable*)	for
narro, narrare, narravi, narratus	tell, relate
nauta, nautae, m	sailor
navigo, navigare, navigavi	sail
navis, navis, f	ship
-ne (*indeclinable*)	(*introduces question*)
ne (*indeclinable*) + *subjunctive*	that . . . not, so that . . . not, that, lest
nec, neque (*indeclinable*)	and not, nor, neither
neco, necare, necavi, necatus	kill
nemo, nullius	no one, nobody
nescio, nescire, nescivi	not know
nihil (*indeclinable*)	nothing
nisi (*indeclinable*)	unless, except
nolo, nolle, nolui	not want, refuse
nomen, nominis, n	name
non (*indeclinable*)	not
nonne . . . ? (*indeclinable*)	surely . . . ?
nonnulli, nonnullae, nonnulla	some, several
nos, nostrum	we, us
noster, nostra, nostrum	our
novus, nova, novum	new
nox, noctis, f	night
nullus, nulla, nullum	not any, no
num (*indeclinable*)	whether
num . . . ? (*indeclinable*)	surely . . . not?
numquam (*indeclinable*)	never
nunc (*indeclinable*)	now
nuntio, nuntiare, nuntiavi, nuntiatus	announce, report

nuntius, nuntii, m	messenger, message, news
occido, occidere, occidi, occisus	kill
offero, offerre, obtuli, oblatus	offer
olim (*indeclinable*)	once, some time ago
omnis, omne	all, every
opprimo, opprimere, oppressi, oppressus	crush, overwhelm
oppugno, oppugnare, oppugnavi, oppugnatus	attack
oro, orare, oravi, oratus	beg
ostendo, ostendere, ostendi, ostentus	show
paene (*indeclinable*)	almost, nearly
paro, parare, paravi, paratus	prepare, provide
pars, partis, f	part
parvus, parva, parvum	small
pater, patris, m	father
patior, pati, passus sum	suffer, endure
patria, patriae, f	country, homeland
pauci, paucae, pauca	few, a few
pax, pacis, f	peace
pecunia, pecuniae, f	money
pello, pellere, pepuli, pulsus	drive
per + *accusative*	through, along
pereo, perire, perii	die, perish
periculum, periculi, n	danger
persuadeo, persuadere, persuasi + *dative*	persuade
perterritus, perterrita, perterritum	terrified
pes, pedis, m	foot
peto, petere, petivi, petitus	make for, seek, beg/ask for
poena, poenae, f	punishment
poenas do	pay the penalty, be punished
pono, ponere, posui, positus	put, place, set up
porta, portae, f	gate
porto, portare, portavi, portatus	carry, bear, take
possum, posse, potui	can, be able
post + *accusative*	after, behind
postea (*indeclinable*)	afterwards
postquam (*indeclinable*)	after, when
postridie (*indeclinable*)	on the next day
praemium, praemii, n	prize, reward, profit
primo (*indeclinable*)	at first

primus, prima, primum	first
princeps, principis, m	chief, emperor
pro + *ablative*	in front of, for, in return for
procedo, procedere, processi	advance, proceed
proelium, proelii, n	battle
proficiscor, proficisci, profectus sum	set out
progredior, progredi, progressus sum	advance
promitto, promittere, promisi, promissus	promise
prope + *accusative*	near
propter + *accusative*	on account of, because of
proximus, proxima, proximum	nearest, next to
puella, puellae, f	girl
puer, pueri, m	boy
pugno, pugnare, pugnavi	fight
pulcher, pulchra, pulchrum	beautiful, handsome
punio, punire, punivi, punitus	punish
puto, putare, putavi, putatus	think
quaero, quaerere, quaesivi, quaesitus	search for, look for, ask
qualis?, quale?	what sort of?
quam + *superlative adverb*	as . . . as possible
quam (*indeclinable*)	than, how . . . ? how . . . !
quamquam (*indeclinable*)	although
quando? (*indeclinable*)	when?
quantus?, quanta?, quantum?	how big? how much?
-que (*indeclinable*)	and
qui, quae, quod	who, which
quidam, quaedam, quoddam	one, a certain, some
quis?, quid?	who? what?
quo? (*indeclinable*)	to where?
quod (*indeclinable*)	because
quomodo? (*indeclinable*)	how?
quoque (*indeclinable*)	also, too
quot? (*indeclinable*)	how many?
rapio, rapere, rapui, raptus	seize, grab
re-, (*prefix used with verbs*)	-back
reddo, reddere, reddidi, redditus	give back, restore
redeo, redire, redii	go back, come back, return
refero, referre, rettuli, relatus	bring/carry back, report, tell
regina, reginae, f	queen
regnum, regni, n	kingdom

rego, regere, rexi, rectus	rule
regredior, regredi, regressus sum	go back, return
relinquo, relinquere, reliqui, relictus	leave, leave behind
res, rei, f	thing, matter, event
resisto, resistere, restiti + *dative*	resist
respondeo, respondere, respondi, responsus	reply
rex, regis, m	king
rideo, ridere, risi	laugh, smile
rogo, rogare, rogavi, rogatus	ask, ask for
Roma, Romae, f	Rome (Romae: at/in Rome)
Romanus, Romana, Romanum	Roman
sacer, sacra, sacrum	sacred
saepe (*indeclinable*)	often
saevus, saeva, saevum	savage, cruel
saluto, salutare, salutavi, salutatus	greet
sanguis, sanguinis, m	blood
scelestus, scelesta, scelestum	wicked
scelus, sceleris, n	crime
scio, scire, scivi, scitus	know
scribo, scribere, scripsi, scriptus	write
se, sui	himself, herself, itself, themselves
sed (*indeclinable*)	but
sedeo, sedere, sedi	sit
semper (*indeclinable*)	always
senator, senatoris, m	senator
senex, senis, m	old man
sentio, sentire, sensi, sensus	feel, notice
sequor, sequi, secutus sum	follow
servo, servare, servavi, servatus	save, protect, keep
servus, servi, m	slave
si (*indeclinable*)	if
sic (*indeclinable*)	thus, in this way
silva, silvae, f	wood
simul (*indeclinable*)	at the same time
simulac, simulatque (*indeclinable*)	as soon as
sine + *ablative*	without
soleo, solere, solitus sum	be accustomed
solus, sola, solum	alone, lonely, only, on one's own
specto, spectare, spectavi, spectatus	look at, watch
spero, sperare, speravi, speratus	hope, expect

spes, spei, f	hope
statim (*indeclinable*)	at once, immediately
sto, stare, steti	stand
stultus, stulta, stultum	stupid, foolish
sub + *accusative/ablative*	under, beneath
subito (*indeclinable*)	suddenly
sum, esse, fui	be
summus, summa, summum	highest, greatest, top (of)
supero, superare, superavi, superatus	overcome, overpower
surgo, surgere, surrexi	get up, stand up, rise
suus, sua, suum	his, her, its, their (own)
taberna, tabernae, f	shop, inn
taceo, tacere, tacui, tacitus	be silent, be quiet
talis, tale	such, of such a kind
tam (*indeclinable*)	so
tamen (*indeclinable*)	however
tandem (*indeclinable*)	at last, finally
tantus, tanta, tantum	so great, such a great
tempestas, tempestatis, f	storm
templum, templi, n	temple
tempus, temporis, n	time
teneo, tenere, tenui, tentus	hold
terra, terrae, f	ground, land, country
terreo, terrere, terrui, territus	frighten
timeo, timere, timui	fear, be afraid
tollo, tollere, sustuli, sublatus	raise, lift up, hold up
tot (*indeclinable*)	so many
totus, tota, totum	whole
trado, tradere, tradidi, traditus	hand over, hand down
traho, trahere, traxi, tractus	drag
trans + *accusative* (*also used as prefix with verbs*)	across
tristis, triste	sad
tu, tui	you (sg.)
tum (*indeclinable*)	then
turba, turbae, f	crowd
tuus, tua, tuum	your (sg.), yours
ubi (*indeclinable*)	where? where, when
umquam (*indeclinable*)	ever
unde? (*indeclinable*)	from where?

urbs, urbis, f	city
ut (*indeclinable*) + *subjunctive*	that, so that, in order that
ut (*indeclinable*) + *indicative*	as, when
uxor, uxoris, f	wife
validus, valida, validum	strong
vehementer (*indeclinable*)	violently, loudly
vendo, vendere, vendidi, venditus	sell
venio, venire, veni	come
verbum, verbi, n	word
verto, vertere, verti, versus	turn
vester, vestra, vestrum	your (pl.), yours
via, viae, f	street, road, way
victoria, victoriae, f	victory
video, videre, vidi, visus	see
videor, videri, visus sum	seem, appear
villa, villae, f	house, country villa
vinco, vincere, vici, victus	conquer, win, be victorious
vinum, vini, n	wine
vir, viri, m	man
virtus, virtutis, f	courage, virtue
vita, vitae, f	life
vivo, vivere, vixi	live, be alive
voco, vocare, vocavi, vocatus	call
volo, velle, volui	want, wish, be willing
vos, vestrum	you (pl.)
vox, vocis, f	voice, shout
vulnero, vulnerare, vulneravi, vulneratus	wound, injure
vulnus, vulneris, n	wound